At Issue

| Pandemics

Other Books in the At Issue series:

At Issue

Pandemics

David Haugen and Susan Musser, Book Editors

GREENHAVEN PRESS

An imprint of Thomson Gale, a part of The Thomson Corporation

Detroit • New York • San Francisco • New Haven, Conn. • Waterville, Maine • London

Christine Nasso, *Publisher*
Elizabeth Des Chenes, *Managing Editor*

© 2007 Thomson Gale, a part of The Thomson Corporation.

Thomson and Star logo are trademarks and Gale and Greenhaven Press are registered trademarks used herein under license.

For more information, contact:
Greenhaven Press
27500 Drake Rd.
Farmington Hills, MI 48331-3535
Or you can visit our Internet site at http://www.gale.com

LIBRARY OF CONGRESS CATALOGING-IN-PUBLICATION DATA

Pandemics / David Haugen and Susan Musser, book editors.
   p. cm. -- (At issue)
  Includes bibliographical references and index.
  ISBN-13: 978-0-7377-3603-8 (hardcover)
  ISBN-13: 978-0-7377-3604-5 (pbk.)
  1. Epidemics--Juvenile literature. 2. Communicable diseases--Juvenile literature.
I. Haugen, David M., 1969– II. Musser, Susan.
  RA653.5.p36 2007
  614.4--dc22

                                2006039100

ISBN-10: 0-7377-3603-8 (hardcover)
ISBN-10: 0-7377-3604-6 (pbk.)

Printed in the United States of America
10 9 8 7 6 5 4 3 2 1

Contents

Introduction

The term *pandemic* comes from the Greek meaning "all people" and is used to define an epidemic disease of global proportions. A pandemic commonly refers to an infectious (or communicable) disease—such as influenza or acquired immunodeficiency syndrome (AIDS)—that can be passed rapidly through contact with contagious people or animals. The term has more recently been commandeered, though, by health officials who also wish to warn against the dangerous, worldwide increase in noncommunicable diseases such as heart disease, cancer, and obesity. This broader application, however, is generous because most health agencies—including the World Health Organization—strictly define pandemics as derived from a communicable virus.

Pandemics are characterized by the way they travel from place to place, swelling death rates in infected populations over a course of months. Some pandemic diseases will peter out in that time, especially if antidote vaccines are found; others, like AIDS, remain persistent for decades as long as they go unchecked. Professor Peter Curson of the Department of Human Geography at Macquarie University, Australia, adds, "Pandemics differ from other natural disasters in that they are more protracted in time and space, as well as more pervasive in terms of who they affect. They often unfold in stages and can produce widespread social and economic disruption."

The social and economic disruption caused by pandemics is in part due to the high death tolls. For example, villages unprepared for the ravages of the bubonic plague in fourteenth-century Europe witnessed a decline in economic output because of their stricken workforce. However, as Curson notes, much of the disruption caused by pandemics is a result of public fears. "Pandemics . . . invoke great outpourings of fear, hysteria and panic, and such reaction is rarely related to the number of cases and deaths, but more to deep-seated emotive reactions to the particular disease agent." The term *plague* still strikes fear in most people, but recently other disease threats such as Ebola, AIDS, and severe acute respiratory syndrome (SARS) have acquired the power to scare even if not all lived up to their frightening potential.

Many pandemic diseases have had a staggering impact on humanity. The plague that struck Europe between 1347 and 1351 killed 20 million people. When it was carried to Asia, it is estimated to have killed 20 million more. Serious outbreaks of the plague reemerged in the seventeenth and eighteenth centuries, and the disease continues to be active today. As the Internet site eMedicineHealth reports, "In the US, an average of 18 cases [of plague] per year has been reported during the last few decades." Influenza pandemics have also appeared many times throughout the centuries. The most devastating occurred from 1918 to 1919 and claimed between 50 million and 80 million lives. If the high end estimate is accurate, nearly one-third of the world's population succumbed to what was dubbed the "Spanish flu." Stanford University research student Molly Billings notes, "More people died of [Spanish] influenza in a single year than in four years of the Black Death Bubonic Plague from 1347 to 1351."

The majority of pandemic diseases have originated in Africa and Asia through the transmission of animal microbes to humans. The disease-carrying agents do not affect the animal populations that initially carry them, for they have built up immunity over time. They may be spread to other animal populations, however, before reaching humans. Researchers assume this is the case with the AIDS virus, which they believe most likely spread to humans through contact with chimpanzees in Africa. The chimps, however, probably inherited the disease from other animals, perhaps prey animals. Once spread to humans, though, pandemic diseases such as AIDS encounter no natural resistance and spread rapidly. In less-modern times, the disease agents would be carried by the infected along roads and waterways, and thus the pandemic would spread over great distances in a matter of months or perhaps years. In today's world, car, train, and air travel allow infectious microbes to reach far-off destinations in a few hours. This has facilitated the spread of pandemic diseases and made them harder to contain.

Science has done much to counter the spread of pandemic diseases. Health officials are quick to derive weakened-strain vaccines to help those inoculated build up natural immunity to the infectious agents. Such quick response can limit the spread and devastation of pandemics. Creating an effective vaccine, however, can take time, so some age-old methods such as quarantine have been used to halt the spread of particularly resistant diseases. For example, health agencies quarantined infected patients in Singapore, Hong Kong, Taiwan, and Canada to arrest the spread of the SARS virus in 2003 before it could become a pandemic. Breaking the chain of transmission is the most important goal of health officials hoping to keep outbreaks of infectious disease from having tragic global consequences.

The most recent pandemic threat has come from the re-emergence of avian flu in 2003. This bird flu has been carried by Asian waterfowl populations for centuries, and it has caused disease outbreaks several times before in various parts of the globe. Its current outbreak has caused severe disruption in Asian economies. Hundreds of millions of domestic fowl have died from the disease or been slaughtered because diseased birds have been found among captive flocks. The disease has spread quickly to other nations, presumably through the natural migration of birds from Asia to Europe and beyond. Diseased poultry flocks have been destroyed in Russia, France, Egypt, Niger, Turkey, Albania, and several other European and African countries.

Avian flu can be passed from animals to humans through handling of diseased birds. The World Health Organization has recorded 253 cases of infected humans as of October 2006, 148 of which have died as a result. Although this is a fairly low number of deaths, some health researchers fear that the avian flu virus—which mutates rapidly—may change into a strain that can be passed from person to person. If this occurs, a deadly pandemic may result. Some health experts even fear that the pandemic is inevitable because the world has historically experienced cycles of major influenza outbreaks that recur roughly every thirty to forty years, and the last flu pandemic appeared in the late 1960s.

Not all observers accept such dire predictions, however. As Rebecca Cook Dube reported in April 2006 on MSNBC.com, "There's no guarantee bird flu will become a pandemic, and if it does there's no guarantee it will kill millions of people." She cites scientists who argue that the avian flu virus is far from mutating to a form lethal to humans. Dube is just one of the commentators featured in *At Issue: Pandemics*. She and the other authors represented in this anthology debate and discuss the impact of existent pandemics and the fears of potential ones. These experts also address the ever-present controversy of whether the world is prepared to resist and contain the next devastating global disease.

1

Infectious Diseases Are a Global Health Concern

Nick Drager and David L. Heymann

Nick Drager is a senior adviser to the Department of Ethics, Trade, Human Rights and Health of the World Health Organization. David L. Heymann is acting assistant director-general for communicable diseases at the World Health Organization and the representative of the director-general for both pandemic influenza and polio eradication.

The spread of infectious diseases in recent decades is cause for concern. Viruses and bacteria carried by humans and livestock have crossed international borders, bringing severe illness and economic loss to both industrialized and developing nations. The growing threat of bioterrorism also reemphasizes the danger posed by large-scale outbreaks of infectious diseases. Only strong national surveillance of potential outbreaks and rapid containment of infectious disease can decrease the risk of deadly epidemics and pandemics.

The ... emergence of severe acute respiratory syndrome (SARS) in China [in 2002]—and its subsequent spread in humans—first within China, then to neighbouring countries and throughout the world, is a prime example of how newly-emerged infectious diseases can cause human suffering and death, have negative economic impact on robust economies,

Nick Drager and David L. Heymann, "Emerging and Epidemic-Prone Infectious Diseases: Threats to Public Health Security," Commissioned Briefing Notes for CIGI/CFGS L20 Project, Centre for International Governance Innovation, December 13, 2004. © World Health Organization 2004. All rights reserved. The World Health Organization has granted the Publisher permission for the reproduction of this article.

and easily cross national borders, defying traditional national defences. Though the international outbreak was contained within a period of four months by a coordinated international response, it is estimated that in addition to severe illness and death, the loss to Asian economies was approximately US$30 billion. Airlines with Asian routes lost an estimated US$10 billion. At the peak of the outbreak, SARS cost Toronto an estimated US$30 million each day.

Like SARS, the majority of new and emerging infectious diseases in humans are thought to result from a breach of the species barrier between animals and humans. Microbes carried by animals, often without causing disease, can be severely damaging to health when they infect humans. Once infected, humans can transmit the infection to others and an epidemic ensues. If an epidemic is not contained by the national health system, the potential for international spread is great. In an era of rapid international travel and trade, microbes such as the virus that causes SARS are easily transported around the world in humans if they are not contained when and where they emerge. They can also be transported around the world in insects, food, medicinal products and livestock.

Traveling Diseases

In 1990, cholera is thought to have been carried to Peru by crew members of an international trading ship that pumped its bilge into a Peruvian harbour, causing epidemics throughout Latin America where cholera had only been sporadically reported during the preceding hundred years. By the end of the first year after importation, cholera had spread throughout Latin America and caused over 400,000 infections and 4,000 deaths. The estimated economic loss in Peru during the first year after introduction of cholera was US $770 million, mainly due to decreases in travel and trade. Similar losses occurred in other Latin American countries to which cholera spread.

In August and September 2000, 33 international athletes from the Americas, Africa and the Pacific Rim who participated in the *Eco Challenge* (a triathlon in the jungles of Malaysia) returned home while still in the incubation period of leptospirosis, an infection carried in rodents and transmitted to humans in contaminated water. Once home and sick, their uncommon infection proved difficult to diagnose. Of the 109 athletes affected, 29 became severely ill, requiring prolonged hospitalization.

Each year airport malaria—malaria in persons working in airports or living nearby who have never travelled to tropical countries—is identified somewhere in North America, Europe and other geographic areas that do not have endogenous malaria. Airport malaria is caused by the bite of malaria-infected mosquitoes that travel in passenger compartments or holds of aeroplanes that fly international routes. Once bitten and sick, unsuspecting humans, who have no history of travel to parts of the world where malaria is present, prove to be a diagnostic challenge to health workers. Airport malaria is thus associated with high death rates because of delayed diagnosis and treatment.

If domestic mosquitoes that are able to carry malaria live in the vicinity of the airport and bite those persons who have airport malaria, malaria can then be transmitted to other humans in and around the airport. Such a series of events has . . . occurred in the United States of America (USA), where a local outbreak of malaria required greatly increased investment in mosquito control to prevent malaria from becoming a permanent health threat.

Microbes can also cross national borders in food and related products.

The virus that causes West Nile fever was imported into the USA, by either an infected human, insect or bird, and it has become an endemic disease in North America and Mexico causing sickness and death, especially among elderly populations. It is now spreading to new areas and unsuspecting populations in Europe and Asia.

Laboratory analysis of the West Nile virus in the USA suggests that its introduction to North America was a one time event sometime during the 1990s, and that it is later generations of this same virus that are now spreading to other industrialized countries. The US Centers for Disease Control and Prevention estimates that West Nile fever cost the country, during 2002 alone, at least US$20.1 million in costs of illness and almost US$140 million attributed to the public health response.

Contaminated Livestock

The recent emergence in the United Kingdom of Bovine Spongiform Encephalopathy (BSE)—commonly known as "mad cow disease"—and its subsequent spread to humans as a new variant of Creutzfeldt-Jakob Disease (vCJD), provides an example of how microbes can also cross national borders in food and related products. In this case beef and beef products, biologicals produced in bovine serum, bone meal used to feed other cattle, and live cattle from the United Kingdom had all been traded widely throughout the world for up to six years before BSE was recognized as a new infectious disease in cattle. By mid-2004 over 150 persons had been diagnosed with vCJD in the United Kingdom, and other geographic areas including France, Hong Kong and Ireland.

Because of measures to stop the spread of BSE among livestock, including culling of entire herds of cattle where infection had been detected and bans on trade of British beef, the estimated loss to the UK economy was estimated at over US$9 billion during the first eight years after its recognition. As comparison, the culling of chickens and ducks to stop the 1997 outbreak of avian influenza cost the Hong Kong economy an estimated US$22 million, while the cost of culling chickens and lost trade during the present avian influenza outbreak in Thailand has been estimated to date at US$2.6 billion.

Animals were also implicated in an outbreak of Rift Valley fever on the Arabian Peninsula when, in 2000, Rift Valley fever is thought to have crossed the Red Sea in livestock from eastern Africa destined for trade in Saudi Arabia and Yemen. Eastern Africa had an epidemic of Rift Valley fever in cattle and humans in the late 1990s as a result of several important factors that occurred simultaneously—discontinuation of cattle vaccination programmes, flooding associated with the el niño [weather] phenomenon that resulted in increased mosquito vectors to carry the Rift Valley fever virus, and forced cohabitation of small parcels of dry land by humans and cattle. The Rift Valley virus is now positioned to regularly infect humans in the Arabian Peninsula through the bite of local mosquitoes unless animals that carry the virus are regularly vaccinated. The impact of Rift Valley fever on the economies in Saudi Arabia and Yemen is still being assessed.

[Bioterrorism] has raised many questions about the capacity of public health infrastructures to respond to outbreaks of massive proportions.

Finally, in 2003 and 2004 the polio virus spread from Nigeria to 12 polio-free countries in West, Central and Southern Africa. In four of these countries polio outbreaks occurred and spread polio widely, while the other eight localized outbreaks occurred without widespread transmission. The immunization campaigns to stop polio transmission in these countries are projected to have cost over 100 million dollars by the end of 2005.

Bioterrorism

In October 2001, several letters containing *Bacillus anthracis* spores were sent through the US postal service to private sector and government buildings. Between 2 October and 19 November, investigators identified a total of 22 cases of bioterrorism-related anthrax: 11 were confirmed as inhalational anthrax, causing severe pneumonia, and 11 (seven confirmed and four suspected) were cutaneous anthrax, appearing as ulcers of the skin. Five of the 11 inhalational infections were fatal. Post-exposure prophylaxis to prevent the development of inhalational anthrax was given to over 10,000 persons who were exposed to environments contaminated with *B. anthracis* spores, and permanent and costly measures to detect further contaminated letters were put in place in the US postal system.

Following this deliberate and malicious use of anthrax in the US in 2001, the perception of the infectious disease threat quickly broadened. Now, [in 2004, with many nations focusing on] preparedness for a possible deliberately caused infectious disease outbreak, bioterrorism has become a great concern in many countries. It has raised many questions about the capacity of public health infrastructures to respond to outbreaks of massive proportions, the best strategies for protecting populations, and the extent to which resources should be devoted to preparation for an event considered by many countries to be of low probability yet potentially catastrophic consequences. . . .

The Importance of Detection and Containment

Infectious diseases are therefore a volatile danger from which countries need to be shielded. Most times they occur naturally, but at times they can be deliberately caused. No matter what their origin, they must be detected and contained rapidly. If not, they have the potential to cause high levels of human sickness and death, to spread throughout our globalized world by humans, insects, livestock and food; and to cause severe economic loss.

Strong national surveillance systems for naturally occurring epidemic-prone and emerging infectious diseases result in rapid identification and containment of infectious disease outbreaks. They also enhance the capacity of countries to detect and investigate deliberately caused outbreaks, because they often have the same epidemiological and laboratory characteristics.

Not surprisingly, outbreaks of naturally occurring emerging infectious diseases occur most frequently in countries that lack the public health capacity to rapidly detect and quickly contain their spread. For this reason, it is in the interest of both developing and industrialized countries to strengthen developing country public health systems. Strengthened laboratories, up-to-date health personnel and reinvigorated public health institutions benefit developing countries by ensuring early identification and containment of infectious disease outbreaks, thereby decreasing the human suffering, death and economic impact they cause. At the same time, industrialized countries benefit from the decreasing risk that these diseases will spread internationally.

2

Noncommunicable Diseases Are a Global Health Concern

George Alberti

The former president of the Royal College of Physicians in London, Sir George Alberti is currently the national director for emergency access at the United Kingdom Department of Health.

The term "pandemic" commonly brings to mind the unchecked spread of infectious disease, but modern health organizations have been successful in containing such outbreaks before they have a global impact. Health organizations and world governments, however, have been less able to thwart the rise of noncommunicable diseases. Heart disease, diabetes, and cancer are a few of the non-contagious diseases that are plaguing populations in both developed and developing countries. The threat is great because people cannot be vaccinated against these diseases. In order to halt the increase in noncommunicable diseases, individuals must make lifestyle changes that involve more exercise, better nutrition, and the cessation of drinking and smoking.

For centuries infectious diseases were the main causes of death worldwide. Life expectancy was short and epidemics raged. In the 19th century public health measures, basic hygiene and antiseptics marked the beginning of a way to counter the scourge, but infection continued to be the main cause of death until the Second World War. The second revolution in disease control came with the introduction of penicillin and other antibiotics after 1945. Effective treatment for tuberculosis soon followed. But then came the inexorable rise of non-infectious diseases. Ischaemic [restricted blood flow] heart disease and cancers became the scourges of the West together with chronic pulmonary diseases and cerebrovascular disease. As life expectancy increased so did the prevalence of these disorders. Chronic mental diseases and the diseases of ageing such as dementias and "structural" diseases also became more evident.

During the past three decades, great efforts have been made to deal with these chronic diseases. Many of the risk factors for heart disease, cancers, stroke and chest disease have been identified. Smoking, known to be a major health problem for the past four decades, is finally being attacked in the developed world, and lifestyle factors (particularly nutrition and physical activity) are slowly being tackled although much remains to be done. Scientific developments, including the new genetics, are being used to pinpoint causes of chronic diseases and to develop more sophisticated organ replacement treatment. Life expectancy in the developed world is slowly but surely increasing, but at a cost. Economically, the cost per head of health care is mushrooming at the rate of hundreds of dollars per head, in some countries thousands. Socially, the cost is an increasing divide in health care and health between the richest and poorest nations.

The Rise of Noncommunicable Disease in the Developing World

In the developing world infectious diseases remain a major cause of death. Malaria and gastroenteritis continue to take their toll. Over the past two decades any advances against infection have been reversed by the rise of HIV-related disorders. Life expectancy in many countries, particularly in sub-Saharan Africa, has fallen dramatically—to make a near 30 year gap between the North and South in some cases. Tuberculosis has surged with resistant forms appearing. In [the World Health Organization's] work in the United Republic of Tanzania with the Adult Mortality and Morbidity Project we have shown consistently over the past decade that HIV, with or without tuberculosis and "acute febrile illness" (presumably malaria), is the main causes of death in adults, with gastroenteritis killing both children and adults.

Diabetes (Type 2) is now emerging as the new pandemic of the 21st century.

Against this gloomy background noncommunicable diseases [NCDs] are emerging as major problems as well. This is particularly the case where economic conditions have improved with rapid industrialization, such as Singapore.

Diabetes and cardiovascular disease are the main chronic diseases to have reached alarming proportions. As [studies] ... on the burden of diseases shows, the whole NCD cluster is a major problem in the middle income countries, with ischaemic heart disease taking the lead. As a percentage of deaths, NCDs accounted for 87% in the established market economies, 84% in the former Soviet economies, 73% in China, 40% in India and 23% in sub-Saharan Africa. These figures were derived from 1990 data but there have probably not been major changes in them since then. Despite this percentage emphasis on infection in the developing world, in absolute numbers many more people died from NCDs in the developing than in the developed world: 18.7 million versus 9.4 million.

The picture now in many countries is one of epidemiological transition (from infectious to noncommunicable diseases) but in an increasing number of countries infectious diseases are not falling, so there is a "double whammy". Even in sub-Saharan Africa where infections are such a major cause of death, we are seeing the rise of NCDs. Thus in Tanzania stroke is an increasingly important cause of death, with age-standardized death rates several times higher than in the UK.

The New Pandemics

Diabetes (Type 2) is now emerging as the new pandemic of the 21st century. It is estimated that there are 150 million people with diabetes worldwide, with that number expected to double by 2025. This is a conservative estimate. Alarming increases are occurring everywhere. In Mauritius the adult prevalence has reached almost 20%, rapid increases are occurring in India and China and even in the poorest countries in sub-Saharan Africa there has been a major increase in prevalence in urban areas in the last decade. Ischaemic heart disease is also increasing, as are chronic respiratory diseases and cancers.

So why the increases and how can they be prevented? Many of the risk factors for heart disease, diabetes and pulmonary diseases are due to lifestyle and can be prevented. Physical inactivity, Western diets and smoking are prominent causes, and strategies for prevention are described in this issue. However, it has taken decades for such approaches to begin to work in developed countries and prospects in the developing world are gloomy—but must be tried. Not only tobacco companies but fast food chains are now targeting the poorest countries. Reverting to traditional diets in urban settings is difficult—but must be tried. Where primary prevention fails, risk factors should be treated. We have attributed the high stroke mortality in East Africa to untreated hypertension. Drug treatments can be inexpensive but still remain out of reach for many people. Even when affordable, care is often not organized to deal with NCDs and their risk factors.

The NCDs are the new pandemics of the 21st century. They threaten to swamp the meagre health care resources of many countries. Primary prevention is needed at the national and population level. It should be driven and supported by WHO [World Health Organization] on a global basis. Action on AIDS, malaria and tuberculosis are of course essential today, but the fight against noncommunicable diseases needs to start today and be the prime focus tomorrow. The current work on smoking is a start but much more is needed.

3

The Avian Flu Is a Serious Pandemic Threat

Tyler A. Kokjohn and Kimbal E. Cooper

Tyler A. Kokjohn is a professor of microbiology at Midwestern University in Arizona. Kimbal E. Cooper is an assistant professor of microbiology at Midwestern University.

Avian influenza (bird flu) is spreading across the globe, infecting wild and captive populations of birds. The disease has forced the destruction of poultry livestock in Asia and has even claimed the lives of some humans who have been in contact with these animals. Health professionals fear that the bird flu virus will eventually mutate to form a strain that can be passed from person to person. If that happens, the flu will likely become a pandemic with tragic human costs. Protecting the world's populations from a contagious bird flu virus is a priority for global health organizations. Developing and delivering vaccines, however, are traditionally slow processes, and thus the threat of influenza pandemics will probably remain a chronic global reality.

A new form of avian influenza ("bird flu") virus is now spreading across the globe and is anticipated to arrive in the Western Hemisphere soon. Although avian influenza is limited primarily to birds, the fact that this flu is spreading rapidly and entering numerous other species suggests that bird flu may soon evolve to produce a human pandemic. According to [one] survey, 56% of U.S. doctors now believe that

Tyler A. Kokjohn and Kimbal E. Cooper, "In the Shadow of Pandemic," *The Futurist*, September–October, 2006, pp. 53–58. © 2006 World Future Society. All rights reserved. Reproduced by permission of The World Future Society.

a global influenza pandemic will arrive sometime [before 2010]. The emergence of a possibly catastrophic human influenza pandemic is imminent.

The spread of H5N1 bird flu presents an enormous challenge to futurists charged with anticipating the possible impacts posed by this threat. The stakes are high. According to the United Nations, a bird flu pandemic could kill between 5 million and 150 million people worldwide. The large discrepancy between those two figures reflects the tremendous difference that preparation could play in facing a global pandemic. Fatality rates will vary depending on the strength of the resources that the national health institutions have in place.

Although the developed world is marshaling considerable resources to combat H5N1 bird flu, future flu pandemics will place human health at risk across the globe. Accurate predictions regarding the scope and characteristics of a potential bird flu pandemic may avert a crisis and promote the type of farsighted efforts required to develop and implement improved protection of the public health.

A Brief Overview of Bird Flu

Influenza is a viral respiratory disease that occurs in humans and animals such as pigs, ducks, and chickens. In humans, the symptoms of influenza include fever (possibly severe), muscle aches, and breathing difficulty. Flu is a seasonal disease in the temperate latitudes, with annual infections peaking predictably during the winter months.

The H5N1 bird flu contains two critical viral proteins common to influenza virus strains: hemagglutinin (H) and neuraminidase (N). During infection, the hemagglutinin protein serves as the virus's fuse. It is responsible for the initial infection and entry of the virus into the host cell. The neuraminidase protein acts like gunpowder in a stick of dynamite; it kicks in at the end of the reproduction cycle to spread the newly formed viruses to other cells. By monitoring the exact subtype of H and N proteins found in viruses causing human influenza, health organizations can determine when new forms of the flu virus are emerging.

The avian influenza (H5N1) that has emerged . . . is spreading across the world, possibly by wild aquatic birds such as ducks and geese. Bird flu has not infected many humans as yet, but for those few recognized cases the fatality rate has been extremely high. For example, in Vietnam, the fatality rate for reported cases of H5N1 bird flu was 47.5%; Indonesia, 55.6%; and Thailand, 65%, according to the University of Minnesota's Center for Infectious Disease Research and Policy.

Precisely how the [bird flu] virus kills remains a mystery to experts and historians.

Bird flu seems to involve humans by direct contact, and the concern is that the process of mutation will create a form of bird flu (or something novel) that will readily infect humans by the respiratory route. That might mark the start of a deadly pandemic.

What makes the H5N1 bird flu strain so dangerous is that, not only does it attack the immune system and respiratory system, but it does so with far greater intensity and lethality than common flu. It can move quicker through the body and is less easily stopped.

Precisely how the virus kills remains a mystery to experts and historians. To date, there have been few bird flu infections of humans—217 cases since 2003, according to the World Health Organization (WHO)—but 123 of these cases resulted in death.

The Impacts of Bird Flu on the Poultry Industry

A bird flu pandemic would have tremendous financial costs. That H5N1 has already resulted in the destruction of hundreds of millions of animals, with attendant massive economic losses, is widely known. Poultry production makes up anywhere from 0.6% to 2% of the GDP [gross domestic product] in East Asian countries. After the 2003 bird flu outbreak in Vietnam, poultry production was down by 15% or about $50 million for that year. If similar declines hit Indonesia, the costs could reach as high as $500 million just in the field of poultry farming.

Many of the world's chicken and poultry farmers are taking steps to prevent their flocks from being infected with bird flu, but it remains to be seen whether—and for how long—such measures can stave off poultry epidemics. Keeping commercial flocks away from wild birds, particularly migratory waterfowl such as ducks (which act as both influenza virus reservoirs and disseminators) is critical.

In the aftermath of a deadly bird flu pandemic, the public may become apprehensive about consuming poultry products.

In addition to keeping domestic and wild birds physically separated, producers of poultry-related goods must also ensure that water and food sources remain uncontaminated. Aquatic waterfowl shed large amounts of virus in their feces and will rapidly introduce influenza into water sources. If domestic birds consume water from the same source contacted by wild waterfowl, chances for the flu to spread to the flock are high. The need to keep flocks separated completely from wild birds may significantly curtail the availability of "free range" animals.

Because H5N1 bird flu is now considered ineradicable in wild populations, it will pose a permanent risk to commercial flocks.

In the aftermath of a deadly bird flu pandemic, the public may become apprehensive about consuming poultry products. We have been unknowingly eating poultry harboring avian influenza viruses for years, but these viruses were not dangerous to humans. The arrival of the deadly H5N1 bird flu is going to change things. The fact that it has been transmitted and caused severe, often lethal, infections in people who have handled diseased animals will cause understandable apprehension and probably some level of consumer avoidance of poultry. Although producers will cull and destroy infected animals, minimizing the chances for any exposure to the consuming public, perceptions and fears may be difficult to control.

Influenza surveillance is an especially weak link in the chain of public-health protection.

Large-scale animal husbandry practices ("factory farming") may increase the likelihood of pandemic. The mass-production methods used by the international poultry industry, such as keeping large numbers of animals in close proximity, could increase the opportunity for transmission. Meat packing, poultry packing, and poultry storage facilities should be carefully watched and managed in order to minimize future global health issues.

Rapid Response Required

One of the most crucial first steps in protecting the public from the threat of a bird flu pandemic is ensuring that health organizations respond quickly and effectively to tips and information they receive about possible small outbreaks of the disease. This information could come in the form of farmers or ranchers reporting illnesses among their flocks to health officials, perhaps through veterinarians. Health officials must act quickly to determine if the illness is a flu and if it is of the deadly H5N1 variety. This is what WHO refers to as "influenza surveillance."

Unfortunately, influenza surveillance is an especially weak link in the chain of public-health protection. Exactly where, when, and (most important) how quickly and reliably the emergence of a new flu virus with pandemic potential is recognized will determine whether a vaccine can be produced before the virus spreads across the world. People and products now traverse the planet with ease, meaning that a future flu pandemic may engulf the world with unprecedented speed.

Proper vaccination of national populations is the most reliable and effective way to limit a bird flu pandemic's destructive scope.

WHO conducts continuous worldwide surveillance to monitor influenza and detect newly emerging virus subtypes. Despite impressive efforts, the fact that the entire globe must be monitored continuously suggests that coverage in some regions is less than perfect. In the near term, the best chance to control a pandemic is to recognize its emergence as early as possible. This will demand resources sufficient to enable comprehensive, continuous worldwide surveillance and accurate clinical assessments.

Quick culling (slaughter) of infected animals and development of new animal vaccination methods for bird flocks are not necessarily simple or complete solutions. Vaccinations prevent disease, not infection. Although inhibited, H5N1 bird flu viruses might reproduce without generating any obvious signs in vaccinated flocks. Bird vaccinations might interfere with the ability of health workers to determine whether or not the virus is spreading, because both vaccinated birds and sick birds could test positive for flu antibodies. It may be possible to produce a bird flu vaccine that allows health researchers to distinguish between these two groups.

Challenges for Vaccine Production and Distribution

Beyond surveillance, the issue of vaccination—developing a vaccine and making it readily available to several million people—is one of great importance. Proper vaccination of national populations is the most reliable and effective way to limit a bird flu pandemic's destructive scope.

One fear among health officials is that a killer flu might emerge and spread far faster than humanity can manufacture vaccine stocks. Also, there is no certainty that a new pandemic virus would follow the same pattern of previous viruses—a strong upsurge during the winter months, dying off significantly during the spring. History has shown that a pandemic could start well outside of the regular flu season. The great killer flu of 1918 began months earlier than normal.

One problem with influenza vaccination as practiced now is that the immunity doesn't last long.

Unfortunately, these fears are quite credible. If the H5N1 bird flu sparks a human pandemic in the near term, world vaccine supplies will not be able to meet the demand even in a best-case scenario. In a worst-case scenario, no vaccine will be available at all; the world will be in serious trouble.

Vaccine production is more complicated than simple drug production: Producers would need nine months to develop and test virus seed stocks, confirm safety and effectiveness in patient target groups, and scale up vaccine production to meet the needs of entire national populations. The only way to ensure that the vaccine will work against the pandemic strain is to produce it immediately after the new virus has emerged. This means significant casualties may occur before the pandemic is recognized and the large-scale vaccine production process can even begin.

The problem, however, does not end if and when a vaccine stock sufficient to protect everyone from H5N1 bird flu infection is in hand. Hopefully, the ability of national and international health organizations to devise, test, license, and distribute vaccines will improve before a crisis, but a sustained and multifaceted effort will be needed to control the future threat of pandemic influenza.

Both vaccine-development methods and vaccination techniques must be updated and improved to meet a threat that will never recede. One problem with influenza vaccination as practiced now is that the immunity doesn't last long—about two years at most. That means that all of us who stood in line in 1976 to get the free swine flu vaccine are no longer guaranteed protection against that virus if it reemerges. Recent research has indicated that under-the-skin injections, rather than inoculation in muscle tissue, may lead to far more effective vaccination while using less medicine.

Existing influenza vaccine production methods are slow, and we cannot rely on them indefinitely. Pandemics may emerge at any time and anywhere and are projected to spread rapidly. Consequently, depending on vaccines that will be produced using methods that will require months to gear up to the challenge is a risky proposition.

Special Aspects of a Global Disease

Influenza is a winter season disease in temperate latitudes, but it is present year-round in tropical areas. If a pandemic emerged in southern China during the late summer months, vaccine production for the upcoming winter season would already be well under way. The sudden appearance of a new and different virus would require an abrupt shift in vaccine production priorities. Unless this new virus threat were recognized immediately and manufacturing processes were flexible enough to shift quickly to production of the pandemic vaccine, there would be no vaccine ready to meet demand.

The constant challenge posed by flu viruses—their adaptability, hardiness, and capacity for change and explosive emergence—suggests that health organizations should focus on new and faster vaccine production methods. Several technologies, such as cell-culture-based and DNA vaccines, have shown potential and offer promising leads for future development.

Whatever method is used to create the vaccine, planners should keep in mind that pharmaceutical companies are increasingly unwilling to produce these vital drugs without governmental protection from liability litigation. During the 1976 swine flu outbreak, there were a number of deaths from reactions to the vaccine. Since then, vaccine producers have insisted that the potential burden of liability, from vaccine-related complications be shared. This could be a significant financial commitment if vaccine is needed for the majority of the population. News coverage of President [George W.] Bush's $7.1 billion budget for avian flu protection frequently fails to mention the potential cost of litigation protection.

Although stockpiling anti-influenza drugs like Tamiflu is an important strategy to augment vaccination during high-demand episodes or hedge against the possibility that no vaccines will be available to meet demands, this is not a final solution to the pandemic influenza problem. If a pandemic strikes in the near term, the capacity to manufacture vaccine will not be sufficient to meet the enormous upsurge in worldwide demand. Influenza viruses exhibit a prodigious capacity to adapt, and it seems likely that extensive use of any compound like Tamiflu will quickly result in the creation of mutant, Tamiflu-resistant influenza viruses. For example, the influenza viruses that were common last season are now resistant to anti-influenza agents used against them.

Tamiflu stockpiling, producing vaccine seed stocks before a crisis, and obtaining more ventilators to support large numbers of patients during outbreaks are all simultaneously crucial and comforting steps, but they do not ensure complete and permanent protection from pandemic. A full-scale outbreak will quickly overwhelm medical facilities and staff, deplete drug stockpiles, and disrupt civic functions.

A Problem to Manage, Not Solve

Despite the rapid spread and potential deadliness of H5N1 bird flu, there is no certainty that this *particular* strain of influenza will actually cause a great human pandemic. What is certain, however, is that several separate subforms of H5N1 influenza have appeared and are evolving in birds. At the same time, other new types of bird flu viruses with entirely different H and N proteins have also emerged. Even in the unlikely event that H5N1 bird flu disappeared suddenly, we would still not be safe, because the basic biology of influenza is unchangeable; thus, the underlying conditions that could lead to a pandemic would remain in place.

Past experience suggests that the sequence of events culminating in a pandemic is rare. As both human and food animal populations expand, and methods are altered to meet burgeoning worldwide demand for cattle and poultry products, we must be alert to the fact that large-scale poultry-packing facilities may be ground zero for virus evolution and transmission. Researchers have also considered that humans will have more of a hand in starting a future pandemic than is generally appreciated.

In short, pandemic influenza should be viewed as a permanent problem that can only be managed, but never solved definitively.

4

The Threat of an Avian Flu Pandemic Is Exaggerated

Rebecca Cook Dube

Rebecca Cook Dube is a freelance writer based in Toronto, Canada. Her work has appeared in such periodicals as USA Today *and the* Christian Science Monitor.

The risk of avian influenza (bird flu) becoming a pandemic is unknown. Experts note that the virus is difficult to transmit and is far from mutating into a strain that can be passed from person to person. Instead of agonizing over the potential threat of bird flu, health organizations and the public at large should be responding to known health crises.

Doomsday predictions about bird flu seem to be spreading faster than the virus itself. But a small group of skeptics say the bird flu hype is overblown and ultimately harmful to the public's health.

There's no guarantee bird flu will become a pandemic, and if it does there's no guarantee it will kill millions of people. The real trouble, these skeptics say, is that bird flu hysteria is sapping money and attention away from more important health threats.

"I have a bunch of patients coming in here who are more worried about bird flu than they are about heart disease," said Dr. Marc Siegel, an internist and associate professor of medicine at the New York University School of Medicine. "The fear is out of proportion to the current risk."

Even Dr. Anthony Fauci, the National Institutes of Health's infectious disease chief, recently cautioned against overreacting if the virus surfaces in North American birds, as it is expected to do later this year.

"One migratory bird does not a pandemic make," Fauci told The Associated Press.

Overblown Fears

It's hard to blame people for feeling skittish. The chief avian flu coordinator for the United Nations, Dave Nabarro, said [in 2005] he was "almost certain" a bird flu pandemic would strike soon, and predicted up to 150 million deaths. The U.S. Secretary of Health and Human Services, Mike Leavitt, advised Americans to stockpile cans of tuna fish and powdered milk under their beds in case of an outbreak. Renowned flu expert Robert Webster has said society needs to face the possibility that half of the population could die in a bird flu pandemic.

"Ridiculous," scoffed Wendy Orent, an anthropologist and author of *Plague: The Mysterious Past and Terrifying Future of the World's Most Dangerous Disease*.

She said public health officials have vastly exaggerated the potential danger of bird flu.

Several factors make it unlikely that bird flu will become a dangerous pandemic, Orent said: the virus, H5N1, is still several mutations away from being able to spread easily between people; and the virus generally attaches to the deepest part of the lungs, making it harder to transmit by coughing or breathing.

"We don't have anything that makes us think this bug will go pandemic," Orent said. "Yes, it's virtually certain in human history there will be another pandemic strain . . . but there's no reason for it to happen now, or 10 years from now or 20 years from now."

Public health officials counter that it's better to be safe than sorry; better to prepare for a pandemic that never comes than to be caught unprepared. Avian flu has killed 110 people worldwide since 2003, according to the World Health Organization.

"Even if H5N1 does not evolve into a pandemic, the steps we are taking right now will benefit us down the road," said Tom Skinner, a spokesman for the Centers for Disease Control and Prevention in Atlanta. "We simply want people to be informed and educated about bird flu. The best antidote for fear is information."

But public health funding is a zero-sum game, both Orent and Siegel note. Money that's being poured into short-term bird flu preparations isn't available for long-term fixes that would, for example, increase hospitals' ability to handle a surge of patients in a national emergency.

"People have been riding this for all they can get," said Orent. "We don't need to make this into something it's not in order to get what we need, which is a better public health system."

Ignoring More Important Health Concerns

And while everyone is nervously watching bird flu progress through Asia and Europe, some experts worry another bug could sneak up and bite us.

"Preparation is fine, but short-term hysteria interferes with long-term planning," Siegel said. He said he'd like to see more efforts at general pandemic preparation—such as developing better methods for making vaccines—rather than a laser-like focus on H5N1. "We're putting all our eggs in one basket."

Flu virologist Adolfo Garcia-Sastre, a microbiology professor at the Mount Sinai School of Medicine in New York, agrees that all the focus on H5N1 may be unhealthy. As part of the team of scientists who recreated the deadly 1918 flu strain, he's glad people are paying more attention to flu but thinks the level of worry is a bit too high. If this avian flu doesn't turn into a pandemic, he wonders, will all these new flu-fighting measures be tossed aside?

"Focusing only on H5N1 . . . I think is a little bit short-sighted," Garcia-Sastre said.

Public health officials always have to walk a fine line when sounding the alarm, said risk communications expert Peter Sandman, of Princeton, N.J., a consultant to the World Health Organization and the U.S. Department of Defense. Bird flu is a tough case because it's both scary and unlikely. People see-saw between overreacting because the potential threat is horrific, and under-reacting because the threat is also unlikely.

"When you look at a risk that's horrific but not likely, it's hard to know how to think about it," Sandman said.

Sandman said public health officials need to do a better job of communicating the uncertainty around bird flu—as Fauci seemed to be attempting this week.

Even if avian flu transforms into a human pandemic, it may be mild.

"It's unfair and dishonest to make it sound like we're sure H5N1 is coming soon and it's going to kill half the population," Sandman said. "It's equally irresponsible to say, because only a hundred people have died, it's not a biggie. It's potentially very scary, but potentially is only potentially."

The Public Has an Unclear Perception of the Dangers

Vocabulary is part of the problem, Sandman said. The term "bird flu" is used for the virus that is now killing birds—and has infected nearly 200 people who came into very close contact with birds. And it's also being used to describe a mutated virus—which hasn't yet emerged—that would spread easily among humans.

Sandman stressed that the current "bird flu" that kills birds is not the same as the potential "bird flu" that could cause a deadly pandemic.

"Chicken isn't a problem," he explained. "The big problem is the risk of mutation, at which point I'm at risk from the subway seat you sat on, or the doorknob you pulled open. After the mutation happens we should both be more afraid of doorknobs than chicken. Before the mutation, we shouldn't be afraid of doorknobs or chickens."

Even if avian flu transforms into a human pandemic, it may be mild. The most recent flu pandemic, in 1968, went unnoticed by everyone except scientists because it wasn't much worse than a normal flu season in terms of illnesses and deaths.

Government officials continue urging people to prepare by stockpiling a few weeks' worth of food, water and medical supplies. But skeptics like Siegel and Orent say you're better off guarding against more realistic dangers—heart attacks, for example, or even gum disease.

"I'd worry more about flossing my teeth than I'd worry about avian flu," Orent said. "I want people to see what the real dangers are."

5

Quarantine May Be an Effective Response to Avian Flu

George W. Bush

George W. Bush is the forty-third President of the United States. He won the 2000 election on the Republican ticket and was re-elected in 2004.

Outbreaks of avian influenza could be potentially devastating to the United States. The president should consider all options in contending with the spread of this infectious disease. Because the best method of controlling the contagion is to isolate those infected, one option is to have the U.S. military quarantine regions in the country where avian influenza surfaces. This is a seemingly drastic measure, but it is one that Congress should consider because the nation must draw upon all its assets to thwart a pandemic.

Reporter Question: Mr. President, you've been thinking a lot about pandemic flu and the risks in the United States if that should occur. I was wondering, Secretary [of Health and Human Services] Leavitt has said that first responders in the states and local governments are not prepared for something like that. To what extent are you concerned about that after [the problematic local response to hurricanes] Katrina and Rita? And is that one of the reasons you're interested in the idea of using defense assets to respond to something as broad and long-lasting as a flu might be?

George W. Bush, "Presidential Press Conference in the White House Rose Garden," www.whitehouse.gov, October 4, 2005.

The President: Yes. Thank you for the question. I am concerned about avian flu. I am concerned about what an avian flu outbreak could mean for the United States and the world. I am—I have thought through the scenarios of what an avian flu outbreak could mean. I tried to get a better handle on what the decision-making process would be by reading Mr. [John] Barry's [2004] book [*The Great Influenza*] on the influenza outbreak in 1918. I would recommend it.

Quarantine Is One Option

The policy decisions for a President in dealing with an avian flu outbreak are difficult. One example: If we had an outbreak somewhere in the United States, do we not then quarantine that part of the country, and how do you then enforce a quarantine? When—it's one thing to shut down airplanes; it's another thing to prevent people from coming in to get exposed to the avian flu. And who best to be able to effect a quarantine? One option is the use of a military that's able to plan and move.

The best way to deal with a pandemic is to isolate it . . . in the region in which it begins.

And so that's why I put it on the table. I think it's an important debate for Congress to have. I noticed the other day, evidently, some governors didn't like it. I understand that. [As a former governor of Texas] I was the commander-in-chief of the National Guard, and proudly so, and, frankly, I didn't want the President telling me how to be the commander-in-chief of the Texas Guard. But Congress needs to take a look at circumstances that may need to vest the capacity of the President to move beyond that debate. And one such catastrophe, or one such challenge could be an avian flu outbreak.

Secondly—wait a minute, this is an important subject. Secondly, during my meetings at the United Nations, not only did I speak about it publicly, I spoke about it privately to as many leaders as I could find, about the need for there to be awareness, one, of the issue; and, two, reporting, rapid reporting to WHO [World Health Organization], so that we can deal with a potential pandemic. The reporting needs to be not only on the birds that have fallen ill, but also on tracing the capacity of the virus to go from bird to person, to person. That's when it gets dangerous, when it goes bird-person-person. And we need to know on a real-time basis as quickly as possible, the facts, so that the scientific community, the world scientific community can analyze the facts and begin to deal with it.

Isolation Is the Best Strategy

Obviously, the best way to deal with a pandemic is to isolate it and keep it isolated in the region in which it begins. As you know, there's been a lot of reporting of different flocks that have fallen ill with the H5N1 virus. And we've also got some cases of the virus being transmitted to person [i.e., from birds to people], and we're watching very carefully.

Thirdly, the development of a vaccine—I've spent time with Tony Fauci [director of The National Institute of Allergy and Infectious Disease] on the subject. Obviously, it would be helpful if we had a breakthrough in the capacity to develop a vaccine that would enable us to feel comfortable here at home that not only would first responders be able to be vaccinated, but as many Americans as possible, and people around the world. But, unfortunately, there is a—we're just not that far down the manufacturing process. And there's a spray, as you know, that can maybe help arrest the spread of the disease, which is in relatively limited supply.

So one of the issues is how do we encourage the manufacturing capacity of the country, and maybe the world, to be prepared to deal with the outbreak of a pandemic. In other words, can we surge enough production to be able to help deal with the issue?

I take this issue very seriously, and I appreciate you bringing it to our attention. The people of the country ought to rest assured that we're doing everything we can: We're watching it, we're careful, we're in communications with the world. I'm not predicting an outbreak; I'm just suggesting to you that we better be thinking about it. And we are. And we're more than thinking about it; we're trying to put plans in place, and one of the plans—back to where your original question came—was, if we need to take some significant action, how best to do so. And I think the President ought to have all options on the table to understand what the consequences are, but—all assets on the table—not options—assets on the table to be able to deal with something this significant.

6

Quarantine Would Be an Ineffective Response to Avian Flu

Wendy Orent

Wendy Orent is a freelance writer based in Atlanta. She is the author of Plague: The Mysterious Past and Terrifying Future of the World's Most Dangerous Disease.

The avian influenza virus has not reached pandemic propor-tions, but many governments are devising defenses to protect their people from the disease. Some leaders in the United States have suggested using the military to quarantine areas where in-fection is discovered. Such a move would be unwise. Since influ-enza spreads easily, confining people together might facilitate in-fection; it also might aid in creating a more lethal strain of the disease. Vaccination, not quarantine, remains the best response to influenza outbreaks.

[Since 2003], a deadly strain of chicken flu known as H5N1 has been killing birds in Asia. While slightly more than 100 people are known to have contracted the disease, and 60 of them have died, there is still no sign that the flu has begun to spread from person to person.

That hasn't prevented a recent outbreak of apocalyptic warnings from health officials and experts about the specter of a worldwide pandemic. In Hurricane Katrina's wake, health officials in the United States are talking more and more about

Wendy Orent, "The Fear Contagion," *Washington Post*, October 16, 2005, p. B01. © 2005 The Washington Post Company. Reproduced by permission of the author.

pandemic preparation. Some of these ideas—such as stockpiling vaccines—are sensible, whether or not bird flu turns into a human disease and begins to spread rapidly.

But other ideas aren't. A few scientists have suggested "priming" people with a dose of the new vaccine against H5N1 before we even know whether a pandemic is coming. Vaccinating large numbers of people against a disease that may never appear carries its own risks. Remember the swine flu debacle of 1976? At least 25 people died from vaccine complications and no epidemic ever erupted. That should be warning enough.

A Frightening Response

Another dangerous idea for pandemic preparation has come from President [George W.] Bush. [In October 2005], he suggested using the military to enforce a quarantine. "Who [is] best to be able to effect a quarantine?" he asked rhetorically at a press conference. "One option is the use of a military that's able to plan and move."

[Quarantine] is an example of a cure that is as frightening as the disease.

The very term quarantine can be misunderstood (not to mention the military's role). Did the president mean gathering those exposed to flu in a single location and forcing them to stay there? Did he mean isolating them in their homes? Cordoning off whole communities where cases crop up? Not all quarantines are alike; each carries its own risks and benefits.

If this were idle presidential speculation, it wouldn't be worrisome. But he isn't the only one talking about quarantines and calling in the troops. In an Oct. 5 interview on "The NewsHour With Jim Lehrer," Julie Gerberding, director of the Centers for Disease Control and Prevention, also wondered whether the government would need to turn to "containment" or "quarantine the people who are exposed." She too remarked that the military or the National Guard might be summoned "to maintain civil order, in the context of scarce resources or an overwhelming epidemic. . . . It would be foolish not to at least consider it and plan for that as a possibility."

This is an example of a cure that is as frightening as the disease. It is hard to imagine how the military would oversee a quarantined area. If a health worker, drug addict or teenager attempted to break the quarantine, what would soldiers do? Shoot on sight? Teenagers and health workers were the people who most often violated quarantine rules in Toronto during the severe acute respiratory syndrome (SARS) scare in 2003. Moreover, the use of a quarantine to control a flu pandemic isn't only a potential threat to life and civil liberties; it's also a waste of money, resources and time. The reason: There isn't any kind of quarantine that will do any good—at least not for a pandemic influenza.

Influenza Spreads Easily

Quarantine, from the Italian "*quarantina*," which means "space of 40 days," dates from 15th-century regulations devised in certain Italian cities to control the spread of plague by sequestering those thought to have been exposed to the disease. Along with isolation—secluding those who are clearly sick—it can be an effective tool for controlling outbreaks of certain types of disease. In 1910 and 1920, before antibiotics, plague experts in Manchuria controlled several deadly outbreaks of pneumonic plague using quarantine and isolation alone. But pneumonic plague, now rare, spreads in a very different way than flu does. Pneumonic plague germs are coughed out in large droplets that quickly fall to the ground. If you are more than six feet away from a plague patient, you're unlikely to catch the disease. Also, plague patients are typically very ill before they can transmit the germ to others. "There is no disease more susceptible to quarantine than plague," wrote the physician Wu Lien-teh, who helped break the Manchurian epidemics.

Influenza is entirely different. The virus spreads explosively. Coughing, sneezing, or even speaking launches flu particles in an aerosol cloud of tiny droplets, which can drift in the air for some distance. Physician and flu researcher Edwin Kilbourne, who worked with flu patients during the pandemic of 1957–58, points out that people with flu may shed the virus even before they know they're sick—not much, but enough to transmit the disease. Worse, some 10 to 20 percent of flu patients have subclinical infections; they never look sick at all. Yet they can still spread infection. Faced with a flu pandemic, you'd hardly know where the disease was coming from.

A strictly enforced quarantine could do more harm than good.

How can you quarantine a disease like that? According to Kilbourne, you can't. "I think it is totally unreasonable on the basis of every pandemic we've had," says Kilbourne. "Every earlier pandemic seeded in multiple foci at the same time. Quarantine simply will not work."

Creating a More Virulent Strain

Indeed, a strictly enforced quarantine could do more harm than good. Herding large numbers of possibly infected people together makes it likely that any influenza strain passed among them would actually *increase* in virulence. Usually, in order to spread, human flu germs need hosts mobile enough to walk around and sneeze on other people. Those flu strains so deadly that they kill or disable their hosts won't get the chance to spread and will die off. This keeps human flu virulence within bounds.

The signal exception is the 1918 flu, which acquired its extreme lethality, according to University of Louisville evolutionary biologist Paul W. Ewald, in the crowded and terrible conditions on the Western Front during World War I. Troops by the train and truckload were constantly being moved in and out of this petri dish, meaning a severely flu-stricken soldier didn't have to move much to infect others.

Vaccination is the gold standard for pandemic preparation.

Suppose that a government official today decided to round up exposed people and move them to a space like the Superdome in New Orleans. It's unlikely that even a crowded Superdome could replicate the conditions on the Western Front. But, depending on how densely packed people were, you could expect the flu strain trapped among them to increase in virulence. You'd be breeding a deadlier flu.

If you let people walk around freely, only those strains mild enough to allow people to stay on their feet would spread easily.

Vaccines Remain the Best Defense

If quarantine won't work, what would? What about medication? Kilbourne is not optimistic about the vaunted (and expensive) antiviral drug Tamiflu, which can be taken to prevent or treat flu. "The problem with antivirals is that they are untried on any mass basis," says Kilbourne. "How long are you going to keep people on antivirals? Also, we don't know about any side effects of the newer antivirals. Older antivirals cause neurological problems in older people."

Kilbourne thinks that preventive vaccines are our best, and only, strategy for combating a pandemic flu threat. The new vaccine, developed with National Institutes of Health sponsorship, shows some ability to protect. But Kilbourne, who in 1969 developed the first reassortant flu vaccine (one made by combining snippets of genetic material from different flu strains), isn't enthusiastic. First, the new vaccine must be given in two doses, at very high concentrations. And it's hard to grow. Kilbourne adds, "We don't have enough if a pandemic happened tomorrow."

Still, vaccination is the gold standard for pandemic preparation—once we know that a contagious human disease is emerging and the risk of vaccination becomes less than the risk of disease.

That's a long way from now. Despite all the hysteria, there isn't a shred of evidence that a pandemic is actually on the way. Developing new flu vaccines is a useful thing to do. Pandemic or not, flu kills thousands every year. But devising quarantine plans is useless.

7

America Will Be Prepared for the Avian Flu Pandemic

George W. Bush

George W. Bush is the forty-third President of the United States. He won the 2000 election on the Republican ticket and was re-elected in 2004.

Avian influenza may threaten America in the near future. To meet that threat, the nation will adhere to a strategy of early detection and rapid response. America will work with the international community to track the disease; it will help coordinate federal, state, and local efforts to combat contagion; and it will fund the development of vaccines to contain outbreaks. The government will also keep the American public informed of the progress and risks of this potentially deadly flu.

Most Americans are familiar with the influenza or the "flu" as a respiratory illness that makes hundreds of thousands of people sick every year. This fall [in 2005] as the flu season approaches, millions of our fellow citizens are once again visiting their doctors for their annual flu shot. I had mine. For most, it's just simply a precautionary measure to avoid the fever or a sore throat or muscle aches that come with the flu. Seasonal flu is extremely dangerous for some—people whose immune systems have been weakened by age or illness. But it is not usually life-threatening for most healthy people.

Pandemic flu is another matter. Pandemic flu occurs when a new strain of influenza emerges that can be transmitted eas-

George W. Bush, "President Outlines Pandemic Influenza Preparations and Response," William Natcher Center, National Institutes of Health, November 1, 2005.

ily from person to person—and for which there is little or no natural immunity. Unlike seasonal flu, most people have not built up resistance to it. And unlike seasonal flu, it can kill those who are young and the healthy as well as those who are frail and sick.

At this moment, there is no pandemic influenza in the United States or the world. But if history is our guide, there is reason to be concerned. In the last century, our country and the world have been hit by three influenza pandemics—and viruses from birds contributed to all of them. The first, which struck in 1918, killed over half-a-million Americans and more than 20 million people across the globe. One-third of the U.S. population was infected, and life expectancy in our country was reduced by 13 years. The 1918 pandemic was followed by pandemics in 1957 and 1968 which killed tens of thousands of Americans, and millions across the world. . . .

Scientists and doctors cannot tell us where or when the next pandemic will strike, or how severe it will be, but most agree: at some point, we are likely to face another pandemic. And the scientific community is increasingly concerned by a new influenza virus known as H5N1—or avian flu—that is now spreading through bird populations across Asia, and has recently reached Europe.

First Outbreaks of Avian Flu

This new strain of influenza has infected domesticated birds like ducks and chickens, as well as long-range migratory birds. In 1997, the first recorded outbreak among people took place in Hong Kong, when 18 people became infected and six died from the disease. Public health officials in the region took aggressive action and successfully contained the spread of the virus. Avian flu struck again in late 2003, and has infected over 120 people in Thailand, Cambodia, Vietnam and Indonesia, and killed more than 60—that's a fatality rate of about 50 percent.

At this point, we do not have evidence that a pandemic is imminent. Most of the people in Southeast Asia who got sick were handling infected birds. And while the avian flu virus has spread from Asia to Europe, there are no reports of infected birds, animals, or people in the United States. Even if the virus does eventually appear on our shores in birds, that does not mean people in our country will be infected. Avian flu is still primarily an animal disease. And as of now, unless people come into direct, sustained contact with infected birds, it is unlikely they will come down with avian flu.

While avian flu has not yet acquired the ability to spread easily from human to human, there is still cause for vigilance. The virus has developed some characteristics needed to cause a pandemic: It has demonstrated the ability to infect human beings, and it has produced a fatal illness in humans. If the virus were to develop the capacity for sustained human-to-human transmission, it could spread quickly across the globe.

Getting the Nation Prepared

Our country has been given fair warning of this danger to our homeland—and time to prepare. It's my responsibility as President to take measures now to protect the American people from the possibility that human-to-human transmission may occur. So several months ago [in 2005], I directed all relevant departments and agencies in the federal government to take steps to address the threat of avian and pandemic flu. Since that time, my administration has developed a comprehensive national strategy, with concrete measures we can take to prepare for an influenza pandemic.

In the fight against avian and pandemic flu, early detection is our first line of defense.

Today, I am announcing key elements of that strategy. Our strategy is designed to meet three critical goals: First, we must detect outbreaks that occur anywhere in the world; second, we must protect the American people by stockpiling vaccines and antiviral drugs, and improve our ability to rapidly produce new vaccines against a pandemic strain; and, third, we must be ready to respond at the federal, state and local levels in the event that a pandemic reaches our shores.

To meet these three goals, our strategy will require the combined efforts of government officials in public health, medical, veterinary and law enforcement communities and the private sector. It will require the active participation of the American people. And it will require the immediate attention of the United States Congress so we can have the resources in place to begin implementing this strategy right away.

Detection

The first part of our strategy is to detect outbreaks before they spread across the world. In the fight against avian and pandemic flu, early detection is our first line of defense. A pandemic is a lot like a forest fire: if caught early, it might be extinguished with limited damage; if allowed to smolder undetected, it can grow to an inferno that spreads quickly beyond our ability to control it. So we're taking immediate steps to ensure early warning of an avian or pandemic flu outbreak among animals or humans anywhere in the world.

In September [2005] at the United Nations, I announced a new International Partnership on Avian and Pandemic Influenza—a global network of surveillance and preparedness that will help us to detect and respond quickly to any outbreaks of disease. The partnership requires participating countries that face an outbreak to immediately share information and provide samples to the World Health Organization. By requiring transparency, we can respond more rapidly to dangerous outbreaks.

Since we announced this global initiative, the response from across the world has been very positive. Already, 88 countries and nine international organizations have joined the effort. Senior officials from participating governments recently convened the partnership's first meeting here in Washington.

Together, we're working to control and monitor avian flu in Asia, and to ensure that all nations have structures in place to recognize and report outbreaks before they spread beyond human control. I've requested $251 million from Congress to help our foreign partners train local medical personnel, expand their surveillance and testing capacity, draw up preparedness plans, and take other vital actions to detect and contain outbreaks.

A flu pandemic would have global consequences, so no nation can afford to ignore this threat, and every nation has responsibilities to detect and stop its spread.

A vaccine against the current avian flu virus would likely offer some protection against a pandemic strain.

Here in the United States, we're doing our part. To strengthen domestic surveillance, my administration is launching the National Bio-surveillance Initiative. This initiative will help us rapidly detect, quantify and respond to outbreaks of disease in humans and animals, and deliver information quickly to state, and local, and national and international public health officials. By creating systems that provide continuous situational awareness, we're more likely to be able to stop, slow, or limit the spread of the pandemic and save American lives.

Stockpiling Vaccines

The second part of our strategy is to protect the American people by stockpiling vaccines and antiviral drugs, and accelerating development of new vaccine technologies. One of the challenges presented by a pandemic is that scientists need a sample of the new strain before they can produce a vaccine against it. This means it is difficult to produce a pandemic vaccine before the pandemic actually appears—and so there may not be a vaccine capable of fully immunizing our citizens from the new influenza virus during the first several months of a pandemic.

To help protect our citizens during these early months when a fully effective vaccine would not be available, we're taking a number of immediate steps. Researchers here at the NIH [National Institutes of Health] have developed a vaccine based on the current strain of the avian flu virus; the vaccine is already in clinical trials. And I am asking that the Congress fund $1.2 billion for the Department of Health and Human Services to purchase enough doses of this vaccine from manufacturers to vaccinate 20 million people.

This vaccine would not be a perfect match to pandemic flu because the pandemic strain would probably differ somewhat from the avian flu virus it grew from. But a vaccine against the current avian flu virus would likely offer some protection against a pandemic strain, and possibly save many lives in the first critical months of an outbreak.

We're also increasing stockpiles of antiviral drugs such as Tamiflu and Relenza. Antiviral drugs cannot prevent people from contracting the flu. It can—but they can reduce the severity of the illness when taken within 48 hours of getting sick. So in addition to vaccines, which are the foundation of our pandemic response, I am asking Congress for a billion dollars to stockpile additional antiviral medications, so that we have enough on hand to help treat first responders and those on the front lines, as well as populations most at risk in the first stages of a pandemic.

To protect the greatest possible number of Americans during a pandemic, the cornerstone of our strategy is to develop new technologies that will allow us to produce new vaccines rapidly. If a pandemic strikes our country—if a pandemic strikes, our country must have a surge capacity in place that will allow us to bring a new vaccine online quickly and manufacture enough to immunize every American against the pandemic strain. . . .

Since American lives depend on rapid advances in vaccine production technology, we must fund a crash program to help our best scientists bring the next generation of technology online rapidly. I'm asking Congress for $2.8 billion to accelerate development of cell-culture technology. By bringing cell-culture technology from the research laboratory into the production line, we should be able to produce enough vaccine for every American within six months of the start of a pandemic.

To respond to a pandemic, we must have emergency plans in place in all 50 states and every local community.

I'm also asking Congress to remove one of the greatest obstacles to domestic vaccine production: the growing burden of litigation. In the past three decades, the number of vaccine manufacturers in America has plummeted, as the industry has been flooded with lawsuits. Today, there is only one manufacturer in the United States that can produce influenza vaccine. That leaves our nation vulnerable in the event of a pandemic. We must increase the number of vaccine manufacturers in our country, and improve our domestic production capacity. So Congress must pass liability protection for the makers of life-saving vaccines. . . .

Coordinating Response

The third part of our strategy is to ensure that we are ready to respond to a pandemic outbreak. A pandemic is unlike other natural disasters; outbreaks can happen simultaneously in hundreds, or even thousands, of locations at the same time. And unlike storms or floods, which strike in an instant and then recede, a pandemic can continue spreading destruction in repeated waves that can last for a year or more.

To respond to a pandemic, we must have emergency plans in place in all 50 states and every local community. We must ensure that all levels of government are ready to act to contain an outbreak. We must be able to deliver vaccines and other treatments to frontline responders and at-risk populations.

By preparing now, we can give our citizens some peace of mind.

So my administration is working with public health officials in the medical community to develop—to develop effective pandemic emergency plans. We're working at the federal level. We're looking at ways and options to coordinate our response with state and local leaders. I've asked Mike Leavitt—Secretary [of Health and Human Services] Leavitt—to bring together state and local public health officials from across the nation to discuss their plans for a pandemic, and to help them improve pandemic planning at the community level. I'm asking Congress to provide $583 million for pandemic preparedness, including $100 million to help states complete and exercise their pandemic plans now, before a pandemic strikes.

If an influenza pandemic strikes, every nation, every state in this Union, and every community in these states, must be ready.

To respond to a pandemic, we need medical personnel and adequate supplies of equipment. In a pandemic, everything from syringes to hospital beds, respirators, masks and protective equipment would be in short supply. So the federal government is stockpiling critical supplies in locations across America as part of the Strategic National Stockpile. The Department of Health and Human Services is helping states create rosters of medical personnel who are willing to help alleviate local shortfalls during a pandemic. And every federal department involved in health care is expanding plans to ensure that all federal medical facilities, personnel, and response capabilities are available to support local communities in the event of a pandemic crisis.

To respond to a pandemic, the American people need to have information to protect themselves and others. In a pandemic, an infection carried by one person can be transmitted to many other people, and so every American must take personal responsibility for stopping the spread of the virus. To provide Americans with more information about pandemics, we're launching a new website, pandemicflu.gov. That ought to be easy for people to remember: pandemicflu.gov. The website will keep our citizens informed about the preparations underway, steps they can take now to prepare for a pandemic, and what every American can do to decrease their risk of contracting and spreading the disease in the event of an outbreak.

To respond to a pandemic, members of the international community will continue to work together. An influenza pandemic would be an event with global consequences, and therefore we're continuing to meet to develop a global response. We've called nations together in the past, and will continue to call nations together to work with public health experts to better coordinate our efforts to deal with a disaster.

Now, all the steps I've outlined today require immediate resources. Because a pandemic could strike at any time, we can't waste time in preparing. So to meet all our goals, I'm requesting a total of $7.1 billion in emergency funding from the United States Congress. By making critical investments today, we'll strengthen our ability to safeguard the American people in the awful event of a devastating global pandemic, and at the same time will bring our nation's public health and medical infrastructure more squarely in the 21st century. . . .

By preparing now, we can give our citizens some peace of mind knowing that our nation is ready to act at the first sign of danger, and that we have the plans in place to prevent and, if necessary, withstand an influenza pandemic.

8

National Sovereignty Is Hampering Response to AIDS and Other Pandemics

Maureen T. Upton

Maureen T. Upton is a mutual fund director, athlete, and journalist covering foreign policy and international sports. She is a member of the Council on Foreign Relations and a fellow of the 21st Century Trust.

A nation's prerogative to keep its internal affairs private has occasionally confounded efforts to combat the spread of disease. Whether by willful ignorance or by intentional design, some national governments have imperiled the lives of their own people and threatened the larger global community in failing to alert international health organizations to potential pandemic crises and involve them in responsive measures. Recent outbreaks of diseases that can easily be carried by tourists and travelers have shown that the security of world health can only be maintained if nations face outbreaks immediately and enlist the aid of international medical resources before the threat of pandemic becomes too great.

It is generally agreed that governments are responsible for the protection of their citizens, a responsibility that falls under the rubric "national security." Today, the concept of national security, and even the idea of national sovereignty, is being challenged by the spread of infectious disease, particularly by the global pandemic of HIV/AIDS.

Maureen T. Upton, "Global Public Health Trumps the Nation-State," *World Policy Journal*, vol. 21, fall 2004, pp. 73–78. Copyright © 2004 World Policy Institute. Reproduced by permission.

The term "security" has traditionally referred to safety from some form of violent attack. A decade ago, the United Nations, in the Declaration of Principles on Human Rights and the Environment (1994), broadened the definition of the term to include access to such basic requirements for human well-being as food, healthcare, education, and the like. Disease, which recognizes no borders, attracts less attention than warfare and civil strife, yet it can be even more threatening to state survival. Three times as many people die from AIDS each day as died in the attacks on September 11 [2001], and the disease has killed more people than all the wars of the twentieth century. It is the leading cause of death in Africa and is on the rise in many of the world's most populous countries. These facts should concern us not solely for humanitarian reasons but because, as the political scientist Andrew Price-Smith warns, "Rapid negative change in the health status of a population and pathogen-induced demographic collapse may . . . figure in the destabilization of states."

National Sovereignty Is an Obstacle to Global Health

Ironically, our notion of sovereignty, which prohibits both state and nonstate actors from intervening in the affairs of sovereign states, has aided the global spread of infectious disease. As Price-Smith notes, "In the case of states like South Africa and Zimbabwe, where there remains an enduring culture of denial regarding HIV/AIDS, this means that the international community has little choice but to stand by and watch the ruling elites of these countries preside over the destruction of their populaces." According to a U.S. intelligence estimate published in 2002, over 25 million people have died of AIDS in the past two decades and 40 million people are currently living with HIV. By the year 2020, it is estimated that 70 million people will have died from the disease, 55 million of them in sub-Saharan Africa. Civil institutions are being decimated, and along with them the economic prospects of highly infected nations. Some 40 percent of Zambia's and 70 percent of Swaziland's teachers are HIV-positive. Up to half of Malawi's healthcare workers are expected to die of AIDS by 2020, and the disease is expected to kill similar numbers of civil service workers throughout the rest of sub-Saharan Africa over the same period. As a result, poverty, political instability, and cross-border conflict are likely to increase. Stefan Elbe of the University of Essex, who has looked closely at the strategic implications of HIV/AIDS on national armed forces, international peacekeeping forces, and political stability, concludes that the spread of the disease may well undermine the ability of states and the international system to manage and contain conflict.

China does not permit open discussion of the [AIDS] epidemic and has imprisoned activists who have attempted to do so.

Impact on Eurasia

The political economist Nicholas Eberstadt has demonstrated that the coming Eurasian AIDS pandemic has the potential to derail the economic prospects of billions of people—particularly in Russia, China, and India—and to thereby alter the global military balance. Eurasia (defined as Russia, plus Asia), is home to five-eighths of the world's population, and its combined GNP [gross national product] is larger than that of either the United States or Europe. Perhaps more importantly, the region includes four of the world's five militaries with over one million members and four declared nuclear states. Since HIV has a relatively long incubation period, its effects on military readiness are unusually harsh. Officers who contract the disease early in their military careers do not typically die until they have amassed significant training and expertise, so armed forces are faced with the loss of their most senior, hardest-to-replace officers.

Moscow, New Delhi, and Beijing appear to be either unable or unwilling to monitor the epidemic, but even rough estimates of the number of people infected are alarming. As of two years ago [2002], Russian officials had registered 200,000 cases, but independent estimates put the number at closer to 2 million. This would imply an infection rate of two to three times the U.S. rate. However, Russia spends only $6 million a year on HIV/AIDS programs, compared to the $6 billion the United States spends. Russia has also created incentives for infected people to conceal their condition, subjecting those who test positive to possible prosecution for drug use. A 2004 report published jointly by the Council on Foreign Relations and the Milbank Memorial Fund warns that the number of HIV-infected people in Russia by 2010 could "imperil Russia's tenuous democratic transition and breed economic and political disorder in a nation already struggling to safeguard thousands of nuclear weapons and vast quantities of nuclear materials." But Russia has opposed the inclusion of public health in the global security agenda of the U.N. Security Council, on the grounds that this would lead to increased interference by outside agencies in its domestic affairs. China has taken a similar position.

Developing nations can do significant harm by asserting their sovereign right to deal with public health issues on their own terms.

All three countries face major obstacles in controlling their respective HIV transmission rates. India's ability to control transmission of the disease (estimates put the number of infected as high as 8 million) is hampered by the high illiteracy rate among its adult female population. China (where the number of infected is estimated to be 6 million) faces the problem of transmission by unsafe blood transfusions in rural areas, where desperately poor farmers sell their blood for cash.

Unfortunately, China does not permit open discussion of the epidemic and has imprisoned activists who have attempted to do so. . . .

Decimating Armed Forces in Sub-Saharan Africa

In sub-Saharan Africa, where armed conflict is widespread, the toll of the HIV/AIDS epidemic has been catastrophic, both on military readiness and with respect to the role of armed forces in spreading the disease. In South Africa, about 5 million people—20 percent of the adult population—are thought to be infected with HIV. Adult infection rates for South Africa's neighbors vary: Botswana, 39 percent; Mozambique, 13 percent; Namibia, 22.5 percent; Zimbabwe, 34 percent; Angola, 5.5 percent; and Zambia, 21.5 percent. It is very difficult to prevent an epidemic once the infection rate among the adult population reaches 5 percent, and five West African nations are near or just over this level: Burkina Faso, Congo, Nigeria, Sierra Leone, and Togo. In all of these countries, the infection prevalence rate among members of the armed forces usually exceeds that of the civilian population by factors of two to five. Defense ministries in sub-Saharan Africa claim 10–20 percent infection rates for their armed forces, but in some countries with over a decade of high overall prevalence rates, the figure is 50–60 percent. According to a 2002 U.S. intelligence report, military HIV infection rates for selected countries in the region are as follows: Angola, 40–60 percent, Cote d'Ivoire, 10–20 percent, Democratic Republic of Congo, 40–60 percent, Nigeria, 10–20 percent, and Tanzania, 15–30 percent. With such infection rates, militaries struggle to replace sick or dead soldiers in a contracting conscription pool. Highly trained senior officers are not easily replaced, and the high absenteeism and low morale caused by disease reduces overall effectiveness throughout the ranks.

As a result, these countries are incapable of deploying their full forces, or even a fraction thereof, on short notice. But the scope of the problem is broader since many of these countries are key contributors to international peacekeeping forces. "One of the ugliest truths that everyone knows about AIDS," says the former U.S. representative to the United Nations Richard Holbrooke, is that "it is spread by U.N. peacekeepers." But Holbrooke doubted that efforts to combat the spread of the disease were likely to succeed because "almost none of the troop contributing countries will agree to have their troops tested." Cambodia blames the U.N. Transitional Authority for its high HIV infection levels; Croatia and Eritrea have both turned away peacekeepers out of fear of infected soldiers.

When the first cases of an atypical pneumonia [from SARS] . . . appeared in southern China in November 2002, no international health authorities were notified.

South Africa and China Mishandle Health Crises

Given the inherently cross-border nature of infectious disease, developing nations can do significant harm by asserting their sovereign right to deal with public health issues on their own terms. In early 2000, South African president Thabo Mbeki shocked the international public health community by saying that he was persuaded by the argument of two American scientists who said that it was not HIV but poverty and malnutrition that caused AIDS. At the time, about 20 percent of South Africans were infected with the virus, and South African public health counselors began to encounter people who had returned to high-risk sexual behavior because of Mbeki's pronouncement. The previous fall, Mbeki had confounded AIDS activists when he questioned the safety of the antiretroviral cocktail AZT that was being used to treat the disease.

"There exists a large volume of scientific literature alleging that, among other things, the toxicity of this drug is such that it is, in fact, a danger to health," he said.

By July 2000, in the face of strong international and domestic protests against the president's position, the Mbeki administration had begun to back away from its claims about the toxicity of AZT. South Africa's health minister Dr. Manto Tshabalala-Msimang admitted to Parliament that Mbeki and other officials had been mistaken in saying the drug was too toxic to prescribe to pregnant mothers. But the government has dragged its feet and, according to Human Rights Watch, the country's overall response to the pandemic has been inadequate: "Access to life-prolonging antiretroviral medication for people living with HIV and post-exposure HIV prevention services for sexually assaulted persons have been severely restricted." . . .

While the international community largely acquiesced in South Africa's insistence on its sovereign right to deal with the AIDS epidemic on its own terms, it took a different approach with China over the outbreak of SARS (Severe Acute Respiratory Syndrome). Unlike AIDS, SARS is caused by an airborne virus that does not depend on stigmatized behavior, such as sexual promiscuity and drug use, for its transmission. While 65 million people have contracted HIV in the past 20 years, the SARS outbreak at its worst affected some 8,098 people, killing 774.

The [SARS] outbreak also served to demonstrate to governments that an unwillingness to confront epidemic disease in its early stages is costly.

Elizabeth Prescott, an American Association for the Advancement of Science congressional fellow, chronicled the spread of the epidemic, which was exacerbated by weaknesses in China's political and public health infrastructure, in *Sur-*

vival in 2003. When the first cases of an atypical pneumonia, marked by "an aggressive form of upper respiratory distress with no effective treatment, no vaccine and a fatality rate of 15 percent," appeared in southern China in November 2002, no international health authorities were notified. "China," Prescott wrote, "treating the epidemic as a state secret, prohibited disclosure to public health authorities and the citizens whom the disease could potentially infect." Nevertheless, Chinese authorities were ultimately unable to control the flow of epidemiological information out of the country.

By February 2003, the World Health Organization (WHO) was receiving alerts about an outbreak in Guangdong province of a rare pneumonia, which had infected 305 people and caused 5 deaths. Soon afterward, a doctor infected with SARS traveled to Hong Kong and infected at least 12 more people, who then traveled to Vietnam, Singapore, and Toronto, where outbreaks ensued. Tracing the path of infection along international air travel routes, the WHO issued an emergency travel advisory to limit further transmission on March 12. Chinese authorities granted the WHO permission to visit Guangdong province in April 2003, and only then was it confirmed that the earlier reports of the rare pneumonia were consistent with SARS. The outbreak continued its global advancement until its peak in late May.

The international response to SARS represents a qualified success in that over a hundred laboratories and universities in many countries mobilized to identify the disease and determine treatment on an emergency basis. The outbreak also served to demonstrate to governments that an unwillingness to confront epidemic disease in its early stages is costly. Canadian officials, fearing the short-term effects of a travel advisory on Canada's tourism industry and business in general, ignored WHO recommendations to screen every departing passenger in Toronto for SARS and were unpleasantly surprised to see losses from tourism and airport revenues reach $950 million, $570 million in Toronto alone. . . .

The fast spread of SARS made it crystal clear that we "are only as secure as the world's weakest public health system and for as long as it takes a passenger to travel from that location."

9

The World Is Becoming Too Complacent About the AIDS Pandemic

Maxwell Madzikanga et al.

Maxwell Madzikanga serves in the HIV/AIDS Programme at the Africa University in Zimbabwe. He drafted the following article with Abigail Kangwende and John Pfumojena, researchers in Zimbabwe; and Karen S. Slobod and Julia L. Hurwitz, members of the St. Jude Children's Research Hospital in Memphis, Tennessee.

The AIDS pandemic is still claiming the lives of tens of millions of people worldwide. Most of the victims reside in developing nations, but industrial countries like the United States continue to report millions of individuals living with HIV. The unending death toll and the disease's incurability have left many numb to the tragedy. This fact, coupled with the media's focus on new disease threats, has fostered a sense of complacency about AIDS that may result in false notions that the crisis is over.

The United Nations, in its assessment of global health, estimates that more than 40 million people worldwide are infected with HIV. There is no sign of relent. Each day, there are approximately 16,000 new HIV infections and approximately 10,000 deaths due to AIDS.

The staggering evidence of the HIV pandemic may be most easily appreciated in sub-Saharan Africa. Here are lo-

Maxwell Madzikanga et al., "The HIV Pandemic: A Forgotten Crisis?" *Current Drug Targets—Infectious Disorders*, vol. 5, 2005, pp. 85–86. © 2005 Bentham Science Publishers Ltd. Reproduced by permission.

cated the majority of the world's people infected with HIV and the majority of AIDS-related deaths. In certain southern African countries, as many as 70% of hospitalized patients are HIV-infected, and in certain target populations, the prevalence of infection can exceed 45%. HIV has often reduced life expectancy by more than 50% and has reversed previous gains achieved by improvements in infant and child care. While the greatest devastation exists among the 25–30 million people living with HIV in Africa, Western countries are not spared: close to 1 million people are currently living with HIV in the United States (U.S.) and AIDS has been reported to be the fifth leading cause of death among U.S. citizens aged 25 to 44.

The Destructive Power of AIDS

This vast and largely fatal pandemic has had enormous consequences, reaching beyond HIV-infected individuals. Uninfected children born to infected mothers may be at greater risk of mortality because of the poor health status of their mothers. Those uninfected children who survive may become one of the legions of AIDS orphans. There are now more than 13 million children orphaned by HIV, resulting in the worst orphan crisis the world has ever seen, according to UNICEF. Consequences of the orphan crisis are many, including an escalated number of street children and increases in crime, child prostitution, teenage pregnancy, and alcohol/drug abuse. Globally, HIV has crippled economic productivity (e.g. agriculture, business and development), disrupted social fabric (e.g. family structure and education) and influenced human migration. Because HIV frequently strikes the major wage-earner of afflicted families, head-of-household status must often be assumed by spouses, orphaned children or elderly family members. HIV has thus changed the human landscape of villages, towns and entire countries.

Highly active antiretroviral therapy (HAART) can alleviate many of the symptoms and consequences of HIV. Antiretroviral drugs may reduce patient susceptibilities to opportunistic infections, dementia and malignancy. They may lower HIV transmission rates and orphan numbers, while improving quality-of-life and workforce productivity. However, therapy is out of reach for most people. In settings where the infrastructure to deliver medicines and care is limited, drugs may reach as few as 5% of infected persons. Furthermore, because therapies have never cured infection, there is a continued threat of emerging drug-resistant viruses in infected populations.

HIV appears in the international news, but such reports must often be superseded by more novel, eye-catching health stories.

Most individuals with HIV are unaware that they are infected and therefore contribute to continued virus spread. Testing is infrequent in many countries due in part to poor access by rural populations to voluntary counseling and testing centers. Stigma and fatalistic attitudes, fueled by inaccessible HAART, also discourage awareness—"what's the point of knowing my status, when nothing can be done about it?" Additionally, susceptible individuals in all world regions may wrongly assume they are excluded from high risk groups.

A Shift in Global Attention

Given the scope of this human calamity, what is the focus of medical news in the international media? Health sections are often reserved for stories of emerging biological agents and biological warfare. No doubt there should be much concern for potential emerging crises. The prion, an infectious entity about which scientists know relatively little, is worthy of attention. SARS [severe acute respiratory syndrome], a condition caused by a virus only recently recognized in humans, is equally worthy. Influenza virus seizes the headlines as it continues to jump species. If a shifted influenza virus acquires potential for human-to-human spread, there may be devastating consequences. Bioterrorism also gains headline status, because the practice of employing biological science as weaponry has unforeseen consequences. Finally, HIV appears in the international news, but such reports must often be superseded by more novel, eye-catching health stories. Does this phenomenon reflect the world's frustration and ultimate disinterest in HIV? Perhaps a general numbness to the inexorable deaths of thousands each day due to HIV begets complacency and fosters a willingness to forget.

10

Obesity Is the New Pandemic

Emma Ross and Joseph B. Verrengia

Emma Ross is a medical writer for the Associated Press. Joseph B. Verrengia was a science writer for the Associated Press. He resigned in early 2006 to work for the Denver Museum of Nature and Science.

Around 1.7 billion people around the world are overweight. The problem has much to do with technology reducing people's activity levels, as well as the glut of pre-processed foods that cater to convenience and a modern, on-the-go lifestyle. High fat, high-starch diets are becoming the norm in both industrialized and developing nations. These food choices are linked to diabetes, heart disease, and other health problems that are plaguing the globe. "Globesity"—the new term for this pandemic—will likely continue unless governments step in to counter this unhealthy trend.

It's a bitter truth to swallow: About every fourth person on Earth is too fat. Obesity is fast becoming one of the world's leading reasons why people die.

In an astonishing testament to globalization, this outbreak of girth is occurring just as doctors are winning the fight against infectious diseases from smallpox to malaria.

Now, a new enemy is emerging in the 21st century—our appetite. Around the globe, about 1.7 billion people should lose weight, according to the International Obesity Task Force

Emma Ross and Joseph B. Verrengia, "Globesity: The World Is Getting Fatter and the Death Toll Is Enormous," *The Grand Rapids Press*, May 9, 2004, p. E1. Reproduced by permission.

[IOTF]. Of those who are overweight, about 312 million are obese—at least 30 pounds over their top recommended weight.

Already, a third of all deaths globally are from ailments linked to weight, lack of exercise and smoking. And perhaps most worrisome is obesity's spread beyond wealthy Western nations.

Obesity Plagues Both Developing and Developed Countries

From the glaciers of Iceland to the palm-fringed beaches of the Philippines, there are now more fat people in the world than hungry people. And in extreme cases, people who are heavy since childhood could die as much as five to 10 years early.

"The developing world in particular is going to bear the enormous brunt of this weight gain," said Neville Rigby, policy director of the IOTF.

"We're even seeing obesity in adolescents in India now. It's universal. It has become a fully global epidemic—indeed, a pandemic."

Certainly the United States—home of the Whopper and the Super Big Gulp—remains a nation of scale-busters, with two of every three Americans overweight.

But there are a dozen places even worse.

South Pacific islands like Tonga, Kosrae and Nauru, where traditional meals of reef fish and taro are replaced by cheap instant noodles and deep-fried turkey tails.

Greece, birthplace of the Olympic Games. Kuwait and other wealthy, oil-soaked Gulf States.

Type 2 Diabetes is the illness most directly linked to obesity.

Soon, China will be the world's biggest country in more ways than sheer population, experts predict. It's a stunning reversal from the Mao Zedong era, when as many as 40 million people starved in the Great Leap Forward famine of 1958–61.

When university student Li Guangxu was a baby, rice was rationed. Now, he eats cookies for breakfast. Shopping at a CarreFour supermarket in western Shanghai, Li fills a shopping cart with cookies, chips, soda and beer.

"I like these things. They taste great," Li said. "I don't have time for anything else. Older folks don't eat this stuff, but we do."

Health Problems Linked to Obesity

Type 2 Diabetes is the illness most directly linked to obesity. A condition that often leads to heart disease and kidney failure, it is blamed for more than 3 million deaths a year. It afflicts 154 million people—nearly four times the number who have HIV or AIDS—and the WHO [World Health Organization] forecasts more than twice as many people will develop diabetes in the next 25 years.

Obesity can triple the risk of heart disease. One-third of all deaths globally—about 17 million—are blamed on heart disease, stroke and related cardiovascular problems, WHO figures show.

Countries with extensive health care have stalled the onset of heart disease into old age. But in much of the world, fatal heart attacks and strokes are much more common among working age adults.

Researchers from Columbia University's Earth Institute examined Brazil, China, India, South Africa and the Russian republic of Tartarstan. They found that the heart disease death rate for adults ages 30–59 was up to twice as high as the U.S. rate, and in Russia, the rate was up to five times higher.

Obesity was cited as a primary factor, along with smoking, lack of exercise and untreated high blood pressure. The researchers described the influence of unhealthy diets as "surprising."

Obesity also plays a significant, if poorly understood, role in many cancers. WHO data shows cancer accounts for about 12.5 percent of the world's deaths.

High-Fat Diets Are Becoming the Staple of Poor Populations

The global trend toward weight gain and its associated illnesses is not restricted to the well-off. High-fat, high-starch foods tend to be cheaper, so poor people eat more of them. In Mexico, 40 percent of its 105 million people live in poverty. Yet two-thirds of men and women there are overweight or obese.

Many factors contribute to the widening of the world's waistline. For starters, there is cheap, plentiful food. Even in poor nations, the relative cost of eating is declining. And the consumption of oils and fats used in processed foods has doubled over the past 30 years.

"One year they had very expensive butter and the next year edible oil came on the scene," said Barry Popkin, who heads nutrition epidemiology at the University of North Carolina and serves as a WHO adviser. "All of a sudden for very little money you could make your food taste better."

Nutritionists say cheaper sugar is another factor, despite the industry's strenuous denials. James E. Tillotson, director of Tufts University's Food Policy Institute, calculates the average American drinks the equivalent of a 55-gallon drum of soda every year, compared to 20 gallons of sweetened beverages a year in 1970.

Increases almost as dramatic have occurred in Europe, and soft drink factories are increasingly popping up in developing countries.

"We never thought people would abuse them," said Tillotson, who developed fruit-based drinks for Ocean Spray in the 1980s.

73

There are demographic changes, too. In many nations, women in the work force created a demand for convenience foods.

"We already are tired from working and we buy only packaged foods," said Bertha Rodriguez of Mexico City.

Lack of Exercise in the Modern World

People spend more time sitting in the car, at the computer and especially in front of the television—an average of 1,669 hours a year in the United States.

With such low activity, as little as 100 extra calories a day translates into 10 pounds in a year.

Technology is changing activity levels even in the poorest nations.

"Telephones, cars, computers all come from the freedom from hunger and fear," Bloom said. "But it's had a bad side effect."

Some governments are taking steps. Singapore schools added physical activities and replaced soft drinks with bottled water. Brazil is making school lunch programs serve fruits and vegetables.

But it's a battle against human nature.

"It would be a huge public health achievement if we simply stopped the weight gain where it is now," said Stephen Blair, research director at the Cooper Institute of Aerobics Research in Dallas.

11

Tools to Measure the Obesity Pandemic Are Inaccurate

Iain Murray

Iain Murray is the former director of research at the Statistical Assessment Service, a Washington-based nonprofit, nonpartisan public policy organization dedicated to analyzing social, scientific and statistical research.

Health statisticians use a formula called the Body Mass Index (BMI) to determine if individuals should be categorized as overweight. The BMI judges healthy body mass by dividing a person's weight by height. Employing this tool, researchers report that millions of Americans—and many more people around the world—are overweight and prone to health risks associated with being overweight. The problem with this assessment is that many healthy individuals—such as body builders—end up being categorized as too heavy for their size. In addition, other people who are genuinely overweight may not necessarily suffer from adverse health risks, especially if they are still active and avoid potentially unhealthful habits such as drinking and smoking. Therefore, claims that the world is suffering from a "globesity" pandemic may be inaccurate if these individual exceptions are ignored by the tools used to measure supposedly healthy human body mass.

"Globesity" is the public health issue of the moment. Southwest Airlines has said it will now charge two fares for obese passengers. [U.S. senator] Ted Kennedy has held

Senate hearings on the issue. The World Health Organization [WHO] is so worried by the fact that, according to its calculations, 22 million children worldwide are overweight or obese that it has advocated taxes and marketing restrictions on sugary food and drink. There is a widespread perception that Americans are too fat, and this is backed up by the official statistics.

But there's a problem. Under federal body mass standards adopted in 1998, Tom Cruise is now probably obese. So is Russell Crowe. Even Michael Jordan is overweight. The guidelines, from the National Heart, Lung and Blood Institute, moved 29 million Americans who had previously been defined as healthy into a category that doctors should regard as being at risk because of their weight. Even more alarmingly, 61 percent of Americans are now categorized as overweight and 26 percent as obese. The trouble is that the scientific debate on this issue is far from settled.

The Trouble with the Body Mass Index

The standards rely on something called the Body Mass Index, BMI, which is derived by dividing weight in kilograms by the square of the height in meters, thus getting a good indicator of weight adjusted for height. Researchers generally agree that a BMI up to 24 is an indicator of little or no risk to health. A BMI of 27 or above is linked to higher risk of heart disease, diabetes, stroke and other weight-related problems. The risks increase especially when the BMI is greater than 30. The problem is what to do with the band whose BMI is 24 to 27. The National Center for Health Statistics has only ever classified those with a BMI of 27 or above as "overweight," but the new standards start that category at a BMI of 25, well below the level clearly associated with health risks.

This categorization is controversial. "I'd rather see a caution zone from 25 to 26.9, where you tell people, 'Don't gain more weight, become physically active,'" Judith Stern, professor of Nutrition at the University of California, Davis, told

Newsweek in 1998. She went on, "There's no evidence that BMIs lower than 27 are associated with significant increases in mortality."

It is perfectly possible to be healthy, attractive and "overweight."

Moreover, there are weaknesses in the science behind the BMI. It does not distinguish between fat mass and lean mass. That's how Michael Jordan can be classified as overweight. Most body-builders, without an ounce of fat on their bodies, will also count as overweight. This is because BMI derives its authority from the traditional method of assessing risk associated with weight, which has been to look at how mortality corresponds with weight. This is problematic, as many causes of death also cause people to lose weight. Smoking is a prime example, as smokers tend to weigh less but die earlier than non-smokers. On the other hand, alcoholism often leads to weight gain, which might be incidental to the death of the alcoholic.

An Inexact Tool

Another important issue in the development of healthy weight standards is race. The standards have been developed from predominantly white populations, and may not be appropriate for other groups. In Hong Kong, for instance, a very small proportion of the populace is obese—only 6 percent has a BMI of 30 or higher—but incidences of diabetes, hypertension and other metabolic complaints are much higher, indicating that for Asians, perhaps the BMI standards are inappropriate.

But it is those athletic film stars and glamorous athletes who sum up the greatest problem with the BMI. It is perfectly possible to be healthy, attractive and "overweight." Waist circumference is perhaps the best way to tell whether someone is overweight and unhealthy (fat is stored primarily at the waist). Some physicians do correct for waist circumference. Michael Jordan's BMI under this system falls to 21. Shaquille O'Neal, however, who has only 5 percent body fat, despite his much-publicized consumption of burgers, still comes out as overweight.

The simple lesson is that BMI is a useful tool, but it doesn't tell you everything about an individual. As for whether America is worryingly overweight, we do not know how many of the 35 percent of adult Americans who the government now classes as overweight are actually in Stern's "caution zone," but we do know that 26 percent—well over 50 million people—have a BMI of 30 or greater. That is well into the "danger zone."

It is interesting, however, that Americans don't view this as a public health problem. In a recent survey by Harvard and Princeton researchers, 65 percent blamed individuals for lacking the willpower to diet and exercise. They may have a point. Studies carried out at Dallas' Cooper Institute seem to indicate that even moderately active overweight people have far lower death rates than sedentary people of the same weight. Even one half-hour walk per day takes overweight people out of the risk categories. The will to exercise, it seems, may be a more important factor in determining health than a simple measure of weight.

Organizations to Contact

The editors have compiled the following list of organizations concerned with the issues debated in this book. The descriptions are derived from materials provided by the organizations. All have publications or information available for interested readers. The list was compiled on the date of publication of the present volume; the information provided here may change. Be aware that many organizations take several weeks or longer to respond to inquiries, so allow as much time as possible.

AIDS Action
1906 Sunderland Place NW, Washington, DC   20036
(202) 530-8030 • fax: (202) 530-8031
Web site: www.aidsaction.org

AIDS Action was founded in 1984 to give a voice to the AIDS epidemic in America and create policy change in the U.S. government. The organization provides informative materials about HIV and works hand in hand with research organizations to make progress in finding more effective treatments and a cure. Publications from the group cover a wide range of topics from policy analyses and recommendations to a series assessing "What Works" in HIV prevention for specific segments of the population.

American Cancer Society
1559 Clifton Rd. NE, Atlanta, GA   30329
(800) 228-4327
Web site: www.cancer.org

The American Cancer Society, consisting of more than 3,400 local offices across the United States, seeks to eradicate cancer through both prevention and treatment. In addition to devising national strategies, the society works with cancer organizations around the world in an effort to halt the cancer pandemic. The organization provides information for the public to learn about cancer and also offers research tools for professionals combating the disease. Many of these publications can be found on the group's Web site.

American Diabetes Association
1701 North Beauregard St., Alexandria, VA   22311
(800) 342-2383
e-mail: AskADA@diabetes.org
Web site: www.diabetes.org

The American Diabetes Association is a nonprofit health organization with the goals of preventing and curing diabetes while offering ways to improve the lives of those living with diabetes. In order to accomplish these aims, the organization funds research and provides information for the public. The American Diabetes Association also presents information on its Web site about obesity prevention, weight loss strategies, and the relationship between obesity and diabetes. Publications by the organization include numerous guides to diabetes as well as cookbooks and nutritional books.

American Heart Association
7272 Greenville Ave., Dallas, TX   75231
(800) 242-8721
Web site: www.americanheart.org

The American Heart Association seeks to decrease the number of deaths and disabilities caused by cardiovascular disease and stroke. This mission has led it to address a number of causes associated with heart disease; one important factor reported by the organization is obesity. The organization provides fact sheets concerning obesity and the increased risk factors associated with this condition. The American Heart Association publishes general information books about heart disease and stroke as well as cookbooks that promote healthy lifestyles.

American Obesity Association (AOA)
1250 24th St. NW, Suite 300, Washington, DC   20037
(202) 776-7711 • fax: (202) 776-7712

e-mail: executive@obesity.org
Web site: www.obesity.org

The AOA is an organization dedicated to reshaping the public perception of obesity. This group provides research and information to the public, government policy makers, and the media that redefines obesity as a disease and not as an individual failure to take care of oneself. Fact sheets and periodical articles concerning obesity can be found on the organization's Web site.

American Red Cross
2025 E St. NW, Washington, DC   20006
(202) 303-4498
Web site: www.redcross.org

The American Red Cross is a humanitarian agency that provides aid for those affected by natural and manmade disasters. Working in conjunction with international Red Cross organizations, the American Red Cross actively participates in many programs addressing the HIV/AIDS pandemic. Some of the central goals of these programs are to halt the further spread of the disease and provide effective treatment for those who are already infected. The organization publishes the *HIV/AIDS Fact Book* which can be ordered through local chapters across the United States.

Centers for Disease Control and Prevention (CDC)
1600 Clifton Rd., Atlanta, GA   30333
(404) 639-3534
Web site: www.cdc.gov

The CDC, founded in 1946, was originally charged with the task of finding methods to control malaria. Since its inception, the organization's mission has broadened, but there is still a focus on preventing and managing both communicable and noncommunicable diseases. The CDC offers guidelines for professionals and the general public on how to behave in order to slow or prevent the spread of infectious disease. The organization also provides extensive research on the ways in which vaccinations are administered, the possibility of future pandemics, and new methods to prevent pandemics. Two topical publications by the CDC are *Emerging Infectious Diseases Journal* and *Preventing Chronic Disease Journal*.

Department of Health and Human Services (HHS)

200 Independence Ave. SW, Washington, DC   20201
(202) 691-0257
Web site: www.hhs.gov

The HHS is the U.S. government agency that concentrates on the public's health and well being. It is the parent agency of other government health organizations such as the CDC and the National Institutes of Health. Among the agency's many services, disease prevention and immunization are a top priority. The HHS manages many services dedicated not only to researching new options to combat disease but also to creating informative programs for the public. PandemicFlu.gov and AvianFlu.gov are the two addresses to a Web site providing information on topics such as preparedness and vaccinations for influenza.

Global Fund to Fight AIDS, Tuberculosis, and Malaria

Chemin de Blandonnet 8, 1214 Vernier, Geneva
   Switzerland
+41 (0) 22 791 17 00 • fax: +41 (0) 22 791 17 01
e-mail: info@theglobalfund.org
Web site: www.theglobalfund.org

The Global Fund was created in order to more effectively provide the funding needed to fight AIDS, tuberculosis, and malaria around the world. This organization encourages working relationships between both public and private entities, offering new opportunities to combat these diseases worldwide. The Global Fund raises money and bestows it upon local groups deemed the most capable of implementing programs within a specific area. The Global Fund publishes annual reports, periodic progress reports, and monthly updates as to how the funds are being applied; all of these are available on the organization's Web site.

Global Health Council
1111 19th St. NW, Suite 1120, Washington, DC 20036
(202) 833-5900 • fax: (202) 833-0075
e-mail: ghc@globalhealth.org
Web site: www.globalhealth.org

The Global Health Council is a membership organization based in the United States that seeks to report pertinent international health concerns to both global and local government agencies and individuals. The council's goal is to provide information to those interested in improving health for individuals around the world. Publications by the Global Health Council include *Global Health Link*, which focuses on general health issues, and *Global AIDS Link*, which addresses issues relating directly to the AIDS pandemic. Current and past issues of both these publications are available on the Global Health Council's Web site.

Infectious Diseases Society of America (IDSA)
66 Canal Center Plaza, Suite 600, Alexandria, VA 22314
(703) 299-0200 • fax: (703) 299-0204
e-mail: info@idsociety.org
Web site: www.idsociety.org

The IDSA is an organization of healthcare and scientific professionals concerned with the prevention and treatment of infectious diseases. The society provides research suggesting how to provide the best care for individuals with communicable diseases. The IDSA also works as an advocacy group promoting sound public policy on infectious diseases. One concern of the society is avian or pandemic flu. On this topic, the IDSA has offered reports on the U.S. government's plans to respond to the flu as well as other methods of preparation. In addition to the *IDSA News*, the society publishes the journals *Clinical Infectious Diseases* and the *Journal of Infectious Diseases*.

International AIDS Society (IAS)
PO Box 2, CH - 1216 Cointrin, Geneva
  Switzerland
+41(0) 22 710 08 00 • fax: +41(0) 22 710 08 99
e-mail: info@iasociety.org
Web site: www.iasociety.org

The IAS is an organization of professionals working together to prevent the spread of HIV/AIDS and to provide treatment to those who have contracted the virus. Conferences sponsored by the society provide a forum for individuals from around the globe to share new research and strategies for combating this pandemic. *AIDS* is the official journal published by the IAS in addition to the quarterly electronic newsletter.

United States Agency for International Development (USAID)
Information Center, Ronald Reagan Building
Washington, DC   20523-1000
(202) 712-4810 • fax: (202) 216-3524
Web site: www.usaid.gov

USAID is an international aid organization of the U.S. government. Program goals include disaster relief, aid for countries attempting to end poverty, and promotion of democratic reform. One important facet addressed in order to achieve these goals is disease prevention and management. Some of the major diseases addressed by USAID include HIV/AIDS and avian influenza. USAID provides programs and funding to aid in the fight against these pandemics worldwide. There are many fact sheets and press releases available on the organization's Web site.

World Health Organization (WHO)
525 23rd St. NW, Washington, DC   20037
(202) 974-3000 • fax: (202) 974-3663
e-mail: postmaster@paho.org
Web site: www.who.int

The WHO is an agency of the United Nations formed in 1948 with the goal of creating and ensuring a world where all people can live with high levels of both mental and physical health. The organization researches and endorses different methods of combating the spread of diseases such as malaria, SARS, and AIDS. It also focuses on issues relating to noncommunicable health concerns such as obesity, cancer, and cardiovascular diseases. The WHO publishes the *Bulletin of the World Health Organization*, which is available online, as well as the *Pan American Journal of Public Health*. Within the WHO, the Pan American Health Organization is the regional office that covers the United States.

Bibliography

Books

Jennifer Brower and Peter Chalk
The Global Threat of New and Re-emerging Infectious Diseases: Reconciling U.S. National Security and Public Health Policy. Santa Monica, CA: Rand, 2003.

Madeline Drexler
Secret Agents: The Menace of Emerging Infections. Washington, DC: Joseph Henry, 2002.

Paul Farmer
Infections and Inequalities: The Modern Plagues. Berkeley: University of California Press, 2001.

Michael Gard and Jan Wright
The Obesity Epidemic: Science, Morality, and Ideology. New York: Routledge, 2005.

Larry Gostin
The AIDS Pandemic: Complacency, Injustice, and Unfulfilled Expectations. Chapel Hill: University of North Carolina Press, 2004.

Jeffrey Green and Karen Moline
The Bird Flu Pandemic: Can It Happen? Will It Happen? How to Protect Yourself and Your Family if It Does. New York: St. Martin's, 2006.

Alexander C. Irwin
Global Aids: Myths and Facts, Tools for Fighting the AIDS Pandemic. Cambridge, MA: South End, 2003.

Scott P. Layne, Tony J. Beugelsdijk, and C. Kumar N. Patel, eds.

Firepower in the Lab: Automation in the Fight against Infectious Diseases and Bioterrorism. Washington, DC: Joseph Henry, 2001.

Kenneth H. Mayer and H. F. Pizer, eds.

The Aids Pandemic: Impact on Science and Society. San Diego: Academic, 2005.

Joseph Mercola

The Great Bird Flu Hoax: The Truth They Don't Want You to Know About the "Next Big Pandemic." Nashville: Nelson, 2006.

Andrew T. Price-Smith

The Health of Nations: Infectious Disease, Environmental Change, and Their Effects on National Security and Development. Cambridge, MA: MIT Press, 2001.

Marc Siegel

Bird Flu: Everything You Need to Know About the Next Pandemic. Hoboken, NJ: John Wiley & Sons, 2006.

Mark Jerome Walters

Six Modern Plagues and How We Are Causing Them. Washington, DC: Island Press, 2004.

Alan P. Zelicoff and Michael Bellomo

Microbe: Are We Ready for the Next Plague? New York: American Management Association, 2005.

Barry E. Zimmerman and David J. Zimmerman

Killer Germs: Microbes and Diseases That Threaten Humanity. Chicago: Contemporary, 2003.

Periodicals

Lawrence K. Altman — "Children Slip Through Cracks of AIDS Efforts," *New York Times*, August 17, 2006.

Radley Balko — "Does Obesity Justify Big Government?" *Freeman*, December 2005.

Francis Xavier Cunningham — "22 Million Dead," *Commonweal*, vol. 130, no. 2, January 31, 2003.

Miranda Darling — "The Pandemic Threat," *Quadrant*, vol. 49, no. 10, October 2005.

Walter R. Dowdle — "Influenza Pandemic Periodicity, Virus Recycling, and the Art of Risk Assessment," *Emerging Infectious Diseases*, vol. 12, no. 1, January 2006.

Michelle Faul — "Fatal TB Likely Widespread," *Associated Press*, September 7, 2006.

Michael Fumento — "Fuss and Feathers," *Weekly Standard*, November 21, 2005.

Robert C. Gallo and Luc Montagnier — "Prospects for the Future," *Science*, November 29, 2002.

Christine Gorman — "Guarding the Henhouse," *Time*, March 20, 2006.

Nicholas C. Grassly and Geoffrey P. Garnett — "The Future of the HIV Pandemic," *Bulletin of the World Health Organization*, May 2005.

Stefano Lazzari and Klaus Stohr	"Avian Influenza and Influenza Pandemics," *Bulletin of the World Health Organization*, vol. 82, no. 4, April 2004.
Donald G. McNeil Jr.	"Human Flu Transfers May Exceed Reports," *New York Times*, June 4, 2006.
New Straits Times	"Why a Global Pandemic Just Will Not Happen," February 22, 2006.
Elizabeth Newell and Stephanie Sonntag	"Global Center Urged to Fight Pandemics," *UPI Security and Terrorism*, June 12, 2006.
Michael T. Osterholm	"Preparing for the Next Pandemic," *Foreign Affairs*, vol. 84, no. 4, July–August 2005.
Alice Park	"Diabetes on the Move," *Time.com*, June 6, 2006. www.time.com.
Elisabeth Rosenthal	"On the Front: A Pandemic Is Worrisome but 'Unlikely,'" *New York Times*, March 28, 2006.
James D. Shelton, Daniel T. Halperin, and David Wilson	"Has Global HIV Incidence Peaked?" *Lancet*, April 8, 2005.
Alan Sipress	"Battling a Virus and Disbelief," *Washington Post*, August 30, 2006.
Gayle E. Smith	"An Epidemic of Mass Destruction," *Bulletin of Atomic Scientists*, November–December 2005.

Rohan Sullivan   "Health Experts: Obesity Pandemic Looms," *Salon.com*, September 3, 2006. www.salon.com.

Andrew Weil   "Is Bird Flu Overhyped?" *Time*, January 23, 2006.

George Winter   "Global Virus Alert," *Nursing Standard*, vol. 19, no. 44, July 13, 2005.

Index